MASTER G
UNDERWATER
DIGITAL PHOTOGRAPHY

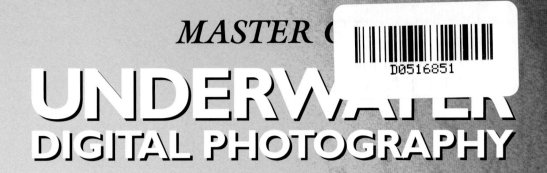

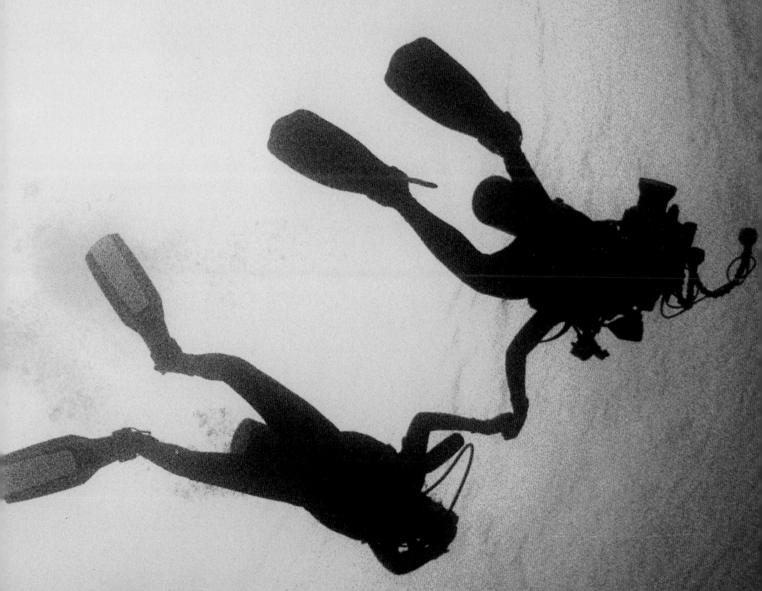

JACK *and* SUE DRAFAHL

AMHERST MEDIA, INC. ■ BUFFALO, NY

DEDICATION

We would like to dedicate this book to our long-time diving buddies, Leonard and Wanda Liggin, who have given us some great diving adventures.

ACKNOWLEDGMENTS

This book would not have been possible without the help of Nai'a Cruises (Fiji), Bilikiki Cruises (Solomons), Capt. Don's Habitat (Bonaire), and Sunset House Resort (Cayman Islands). We would also like to thank all the digital-camera and housing manufacturers who loaned us equipment for our underwater testing. Most importantly, our thanks go to Brooks Institute of Photography for giving us our roots in photography.

Published by:
Amherst Media, Inc.
P.O. Box 586
Buffalo, N.Y. 14226
Fax: 716-874-4508
www.AmherstMedia.com

Publisher: Craig Alesse
Senior Editor/Production Manager: Michelle Perkins
Assistant Editor: Barbara A. Lynch-Johnt
Editorial Assistance: Carey A. Maines

ISBN-13: 978-1-58428-166-5
Library of Congress Control Number: 2004113082

Printed in Korea.
10 9 8 7 6 5 4 3 2 1

Table of Contents

1. The Evolution of Underwater Photography 6

2. How the Underwater Environment
Affects Photography .8
The Challenges 8
   Light Loss 8
   Backscatter 8
   Water Temperature 9
   Currents 10
   Humidity and Corrosion 10
So . . . Why Bother?! 11

3. Taking the Plunge 12
Film *vs.* Digital 13
   Advantages of a Digital Camera 13
   Advantages of a Film Camera System 15
Underwater Flash 18
Accessory Lenses 18
Flashlights 19
Camera Brackets and Arms 20
Face Mask 21
Web Help 22

4. Digital-Camera Components 23
Camera Parts 23
LCD Display 25
Buttons, Buttons, and More Buttons 25
Chip Component 25
Batteries 26
Memory Cards 27

5. Digital-Camera Menu Controls 28
Default is Good 28
White Balance 28
ISO Speeds 30
Flash 31
Sharpness 32
Contrast 32
Saturation 33

Exposure 33
   Exposure Compensation 33
   Exposure Bracket .34
Focusing 35
   Focus Brackets 35
   Continuous Focus 35
   Close-up Mode 35
   Super Macro Mode 36
Continuous-Shooting Mode 36
Resolution 37
File Compression 37
Accessory Lenses 37
Sound Record 37
EXIF Histogram Playback 37
Custom Presets 38
Noise Reduction 38
Panorama 38
Black & White or Sepia 38
Composition Grid .39
Video 39
File Naming 39
Digital *vs.* Optical Zoom 40
LCD Monitor Control 40
Real-Time Manual Exposure 40
Setup Menus 40

6. Making Your First Dive
with Your Digital Camera 41
Practice Topside First 41
Adding the Housing 41
Housing Maintenance 41
Let's Go Diving! 43
Using the Flash 43
Should You Delete the Images? 44

7. Getting Good Exposures 46
Testing 46
The Blooming Effect 47
Photographic Exposure 101 48
   Aperture 48

Shutter Speed 48

Halving and Doubling 49

ISO Rating 49

Exposure Modes 49

Program Mode 49

Aperture-Priority Mode 50

Shutter-Priority Mode 51

Manual Exposure Mode 53

8. Available-Light Photography 54

Exposure Methods 54

Point of View 55

Other Available-Light Options 56

Shallow Water 59

Deep Water 59

Flashlights as Props 60

9. Flash Photography 61

TTL, Digital, Auto, Manual 62

TTL (Through the Lens) 62

Digital 63

Auto 63

Manual 63

Flash Sync 63

Tips and Tricks for Using Flash 64

TTL Housing Control Boards 65

Batteries 65

Flash Recycle Time 65

Single Flash 66

Twin Flash 66

Wide-Angle Flash 67

Slave Flash 68

Flash Arms and Camera Trays 69

10. Wide-Angle Photography 70

Digital Lens Configuration 70

Wet Lenses 71

Reducing the Water Column 71

Camera Angles 72

Perspective Applications 73

Shipwrecks 74

Working with Models 75

Self Portrait 75

Panoramic Reef Images 76

11. Fish Photography 78

Film Photography 78

Lens and Camera Choices 78

Film Choices 79

Digital Photography 80

Point & Shoot 80

Digital SLR 81

Flash Considerations 82

Techniques for Photographing Fish 84

12. Close-up Photography 86

Close-up Terminology 86

Close-up Equipment 87

Extension Tubes and Framers 87

SLR Macro Lenses 88

Plus Diopters 88

Digital Point & Shoot Close-Ups 89

Single and Double Flash 90

High Speed Macro Flash 90

Depth of Field 91

Digital Point & Shoot 92

Subject Angles 92

Software Solutions 93

13. Super Macro 94

What is Super Macro? 94

Shooting Beyond 1:1 94

Tele-extenders 96

Diopters 96

Point & Shoot Super Macro 97

Wet-Lens Super Macro 97

ISO Considerations 98

Adding Auxiliary Lights 98

Face-Mask Configurations 99

Software Magnification 99

14. Backscatter 100

Anatomy of a Backscatter Particle 100

Causes of Backscatter 100

Flash Too Close to the Camera 100

Subject Too Far From the Camera Lens ...101

Lighting Contrast 102

Extreme Backscatter 104

When All Else Fails 106

15. Composition 107
Positive Composition 107
    Rule of Thirds 107
    Lines Leading to a Point 108
    Color 109
    Negative Space 109
    Letter Composition 110
    Opposites Attract 110
    Point of View 110
    Patterns and Shapes 111
    Framing 111
    Cropping 111
Negative Composition .111
    Busy Scenes 112
    Subject Too Close to the Edge 112
    Light Traps 112
    Lacking Contrast, Color, or Sharpness 113

16. Reef Protection and Photographic Ethics . . .114
Buoyancy Skills 114
The Dead Zone 115
Time Outs 115
Photographic Ethics 115
Rules of Respect 116

17. Traveling with Your Camera 117
Analyze The Dive Location 117
Backup Systems 117
Storing Your Images 117
Advance Testing 118
Instruction Manuals 118
Packing Your Gear 118
Film and X-Ray Machines 118
Luggage and Weight Restrictions 119
Insurance 119
Check Again 119

18. Care of Your Underwater Equipment 120
Maintenance of O-rings 120
Greasing O-rings 120
Keep it Dry 121
Camera Rinse Tanks 121

19. The Future of Underwater Photography 122

20. Appendix 123

Index 124

ABOUT THE AUTHORS

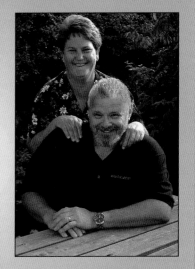

Jack and Sue Drafahl are a husband and wife team of professional photojournalists, lecturers, and multimedia producers. For over thirty years, their articles have appeared in *Petersen's PHOTOgraphic, Rangefinder, Sport Diver, Skin Diver, Dive Training, Diver, National Wildlife Federation,* and *National Geographic World Magazine.* They have been actively involved in the digital transition since the early '80s and are software and hardware Beta testers for companies like Adobe, Applied Science Fiction, Corel, Kodak, and Ulead Systems.

Jack and Sue started their professional photographic careers at Brooks Institute of Photography in Santa Barbara, CA, where Jack later started the audio visual department. Both are active scuba divers, receiving their diving certification in the early '70s. Jack and Sue were awarded Divers of the Year from Beneath the Sea, and Sue is an inaugural member of the Women Divers Hall of Fame.

Jack and Sue make their home on the Oregon coast and enjoy teaching seminars worldwide on all aspects of photography, both topside and underwater. Recently, they have put their years of photographic experience to use designing the Oregon Coast Digital Center, an enhanced learning facility that features in-depth digital classes to help students better understand the digital realm. In addition to their various monthly articles, Jack and Sue are authors of *Digital Imaging for the Underwater Photographer, Photo Salvage with Adobe Photoshop, Step-by-Step Digital Photography, Advanced Digital Camera Techniques,* and *Plug-ins for Adobe Photoshop,* all from Amherst Media.

For more on the authors, please visit www.jackandsuedrafahl.com.

1. The Evolution of Underwater Photography

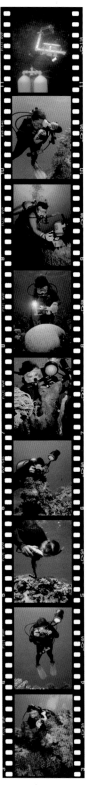

For more than 150 years, the method for recording the underwater world was with silver halide crystals, otherwise known as film. Then, around the turn of the twenty-first century, the whole photo industry took a dramatic turn with the introduction of digital. It wasn't long before digital cameras moved from topside photography into underwater housings so they could be used to document the wonders of the sea. No single technology has had more impact on underwater photography.

Change in the film world moved slowly. New advancements in film, cameras, lenses, and flash systems took years to become fully accepted as tools for underwater photography. In fact, when a new film camera was introduced, it was conceivably two to three years before a compatible housing would be introduced. Then, that camera and housing combination would be in the mainstream for years. The digital world, on the other hand, moves ahead at such a clip that it is often difficult to stay ahead of it all. Digital point & shoot camera models are commonly replaced within a year and the life span of digital SLR camera models isn't more than two to three years. For this reason, we now find that underwater housings are being introduced within weeks of the announcement of their corresponding digital cameras (if not simultaneously!).

Even photographic terminology has changed. We are now starting to see manufacturers refer to film shooting as "analog" photography. In the year 2000, we also started to see a definite reduction of new film emulsions introduced by film manufacturers. Simultaneously, these same manufacturers started to introduce an expansive offering of digital cameras. The Kodak slide projector disappeared, and E-6 processing was harder to find as it dropped below 1 percent of the images processed. The inkjet printer quality quickly surpassed photographic quality, and now photographers could even print their own images at home.

Does this mean the end to the film camera? Not really, it just means that the film camera is no longer the dominant method used for taking pictures topside or underwater. Even so, many underwater photographers are reluctant to make the transition to digital. They have made a considerable investment in their underwater film-camera systems and are satisfied, since they have worked well for many years. Some feel that investing in a new underwater digital camera system may not be very practical because of the added cost and time required to master the new systems.

This causes the field of underwater digital photography to be divided into two groups. You have underwater photographers who willingly sell their film camera systems and embrace digital with open arms. These digital camera users are now the predominant group, and the numbers continue to steadily grow. The second group consists of film photographers who have converted to digital via the film scanner. They have the advantage of using film's wide exposure latitude, yet they can still become a part of the digital world. Properly exposed, scanned-film images can equal or better their digital counterparts and, best of all, you still have the tangible images.

The bottom line is that, generally, *all* underwater photographers today are digital photographers—whether they want to admit it or not. They have all entered the digital realm either via the digital camera or because their film images have been converted to digital files. In fact, we wrote an entire book (*Digital Imaging for the Underwater Photographer*, from Amherst Media) designed to help underwater photographers enter the computer imaging world.

This book is different in that it *only* covers underwater digital camera techniques. We designed this book to encompass all levels and types of underwater photography, whether the images come from a digital camera or via a film scanner. The examples used to illustrate different underwater photography techniques will be from both digital cameras and scanned film. When it comes right down to it, backscatter is backscatter, and a lighting ratio is a lighting ratio, no matter what medium you use to capture the image.

We have over 35 years of underwater photography experience that encompasses both film and digital camera systems. It is these past experiences that enable us to bring new digital techniques to our readers. You will find that when a chapter refers specifically to digital camera problems and techniques, it will be illustrated using only digital camera images. The rest of the images in the book have either been taken digitally or introduced to the digital world via the scanner. We just selected images that we felt best illustrated our point.

Welcome to the fascinating world of digital underwater photography!

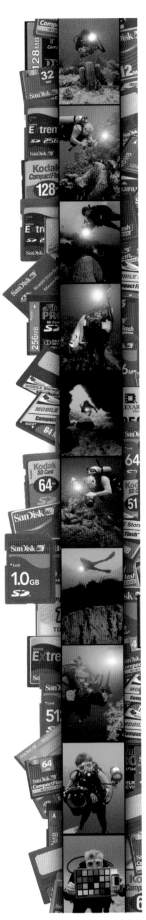

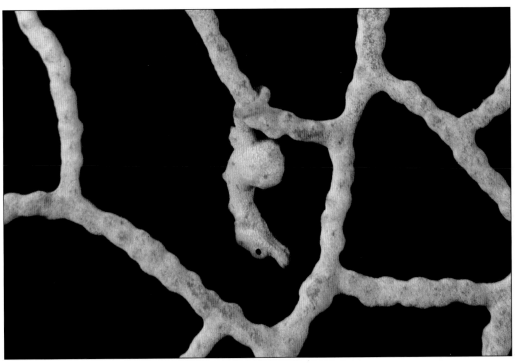

This extreme close-up of a pygmy seahorse (above) was photographed in the Solomon Islands with a digital SLR camera and a 105mm macro lens (effective focal length of 150mm on film).

The two strips of images shown here span our underwater photography career—from the first 35 years of underwater photography using film cameras (facing page) to the last five years of underwater photography with digital cameras (right).

2. How the Underwater Environment Affects Photography

Of all the different types of photography, taking pictures underwater is one of the most difficult. Photography itself is difficult enough, as you must contend with achieving correct exposure, accurate focus, controlling subject movement, attaining pleasing color balance, and dealing with varying light levels. More often than not, the image you saw in the viewfinder only vaguely resembles the final image. When you also cross the line from photographing in the "air" environment to that of the "water" world, it becomes even more difficult. The line that divides the wet and dry environments brings with it a whole new set of parameters that affect your picture. This is why underwater photographers are a rare breed.

■ THE CHALLENGES

Light Loss. Let's explore a couple of the challenges involved in underwater photography, starting with light itself. When sunlight passes through the surface of water, much of it is reflected back upwards, thus the amount of light that continues underwater is reduced. The lower the sun is in the sky, the more light is reflected off the water's surface. In order to achieve the maximum light level for your underwater photography, the best shooting times are between 10AM and 2PM. As you descend below the waves into the abyss, the light level decreases at an exponential rate. Even at a depth of 100 feet, the light is at an extremely low level.

In addition to this problem, the colors that make up the spectrum of light decrease at varying rates. Red is lost first, and disappears in as little as 15 feet. It is closely followed by orange, yellow, green, and finally blue. This imbalance in the color spectrum causes havoc with images taken underwater using available light.

That is why so many underwater images are taken using electronic flash. Even when a photographer uses a large flash, though, the color and intensity of the flash fall off drastically with distance. Usually, the strobe's impact dissipates if the flash-to-subject distance is more than eight feet. In addition to the loss of color and intensity, there is also a contrast and color-saturation loss as the subject's distance increases from the camera and flash.

Backscatter. If all of that were not discouraging enough, the underwater world also has its own unique problem. As particulate matter floats through the water with the currents, it takes on the appearance of snow in

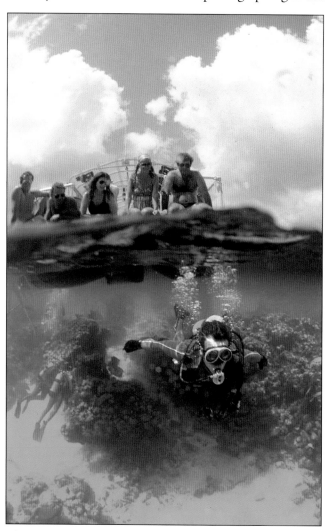

This split image illustrates the immediate loss of light, even when lighting conditions are ideal. (San Salvador, Bahamas; Nikonos film camera)

a snowstorm when illuminated by a flash or other bright light source. This unique effect is called backscatter and is one of the biggest issues plaguing underwater photographers. It's such a problem that we have devoted an entire chapter to tips on eliminating or avoiding backscatter.

Water Temperature. The temperature of the water itself can add to the difficulty of taking pictures underwater. Water temperatures can range from a comfort-

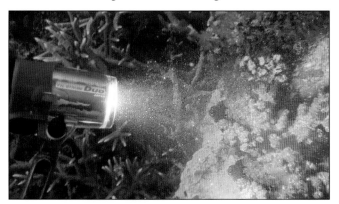

One of the biggest problems underwater is backscatter. By including the flash in the photo, the highlighted backscatter is very evident. You can see that it decreases in intensity as the flash distance increases and beam angle widens.

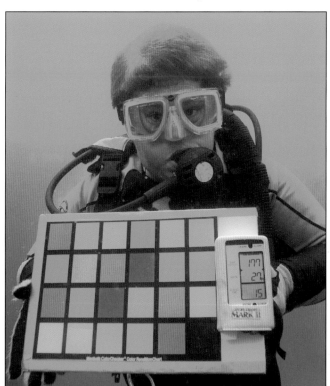

able 85 degrees Fahrenheit to a freezing 33 degrees. As the water becomes colder, the photographer must wear heavier wet suits to combat the cold. As these wet suits increase in thickness, you must add even more lead weight to counterbalance the buoyancy of the suit. Then you must wear gloves to stay warm, but these make camera adjustments very cumbersome. While the

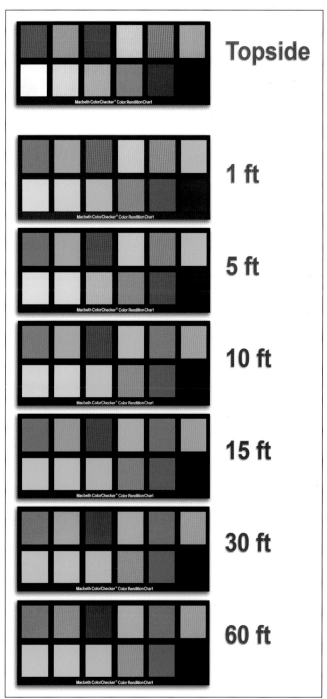

LEFT—Digital image of Sue with a test chart designed to measure the different levels of color falloff at various depths. RIGHT—This shows the final results of all our color chart tests. You will see that when the chart is placed even just one foot underwater, the color loss begins. At 15 feet, red is almost gone, and the color changes from 30 feet to 60 feet are barely noticeable.

popular dry suits offer another choice when cold-water diving, they still restrict your ability to take pictures underwater.

Currents. Are we beginning to mildly discourage you from underwater photography? Wait, we're not done yet! Many of the best diving locations in the world can have mild to strong currents that make it difficult for you to remain stationary long enough to take your picture. With the new environmental concerns about getting too close to the reef, photography in currents becomes very difficult at best. Even when the currents aren't running, the larger camera systems are bulky and can often cause drag as you maneuver through water.

Humidity and Corrosion. The salt air and humidity are other parts of the equation working against you. Salt water is very corrosive, and can quickly damage both film and digital cameras if even just a couple of drops get in the wrong place. Most tropical climates

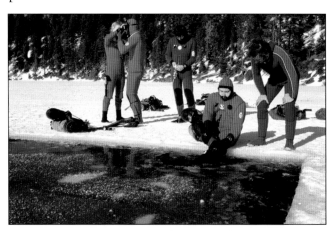 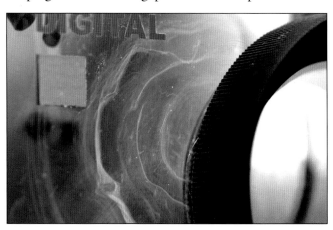

LEFT—Divers prepare to descend into a 33-degree mountain lake in Oregon. The cold water requires extremely thick dry suits and cumbersome gloves, making photography difficult. RIGHT—Small particles of moisture can vaporize in the housing as the digital camera heats up during a dive. This cloud eventually fogs the camera lens, making photography impossible.

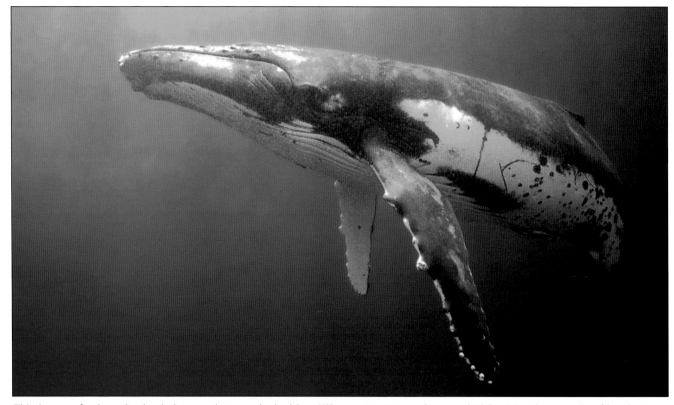

This image of a humpback whale was photographed with a Nikonos 5, a 15mm lens, and ISO 400 color-negative film that was later converted to digital using a film scanner.

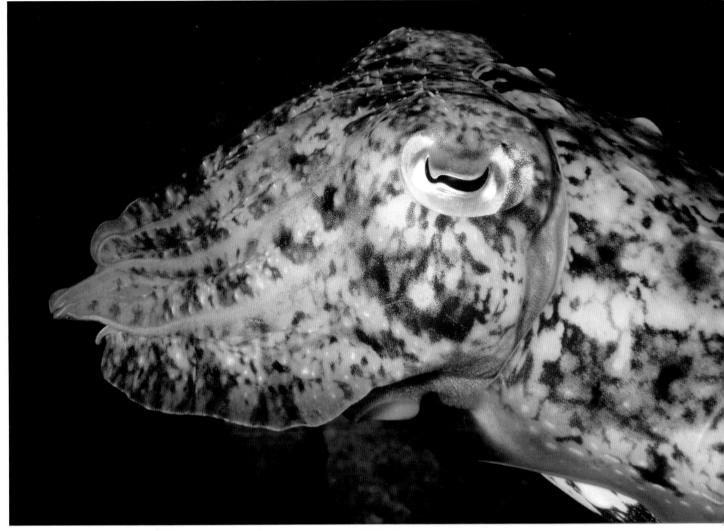

Using a digital SLR camera and a 60mm macro lens (effective focal length of 90mm on film) allows you to capture larger animals like this cuttlefish.

have high humidity which gets trapped inside the camera housing as you make your dive. As the camera batteries heat up, moisture forms small clouds inside your camera housing.

◼ SO . . . WHY BOTHER?!

Whew! With all of these environmental factors against you, why would anyone go to the trouble and expense of taking pictures underwater?

The answer is apparent the first time you come face to face with a 40-ton humpback whale, or a tiny timid seahorse seeking camouflage in the soft coral. Or, it might be the intrigue and challenge of the cuttlefish

that changes shape and color just to escape capture by the underwater camera. All of us underwater photographers are fascinated with the awe and mystery of the underwater world and long to share our experiences with family and friends—even the entire world.

That's what this book is about. We want to help you learn new digital photography skills and hone your techniques. We just thought we should mention the dark side of underwater photography—to make sure you were a team player before moving ahead to the fun part. So, take a deep breath and hang on tight, because here we go!

3. Taking the Plunge

Before you purchase your first digital underwater photography system, you need to understand the basic components to know how they will best suit your shooting needs. Most underwater photography systems consist of a camera, lens, flash, and a bracket system to support all the components. The main difference between film and digital is the camera itself, as most of the remaining components are the same for both systems.

When considering a camera purchase, the best place to start is with a self analysis of what you are planning to do with your pictures. Since everyone has a different agenda for their final images, it makes sense that you match the camera system to your final product. The diver who wants to shoot images for a scrapbook just so they can show their underwater images to friends will probably be happy with a lower-end point & shoot camera system. The more serious photographer, who wants to make enlargements, enter photo contests, or submit images to magazines, might consider a mid-range to high-end point & shoot system. Professional photographers would probably want to use both high-end point & shoot and SLR systems in order to have the most creative control—and the best possible image quality.

The key is to make a list of your needs regarding print output size, lens focal length, system adaptability, favorite subjects to photograph, and then match it to

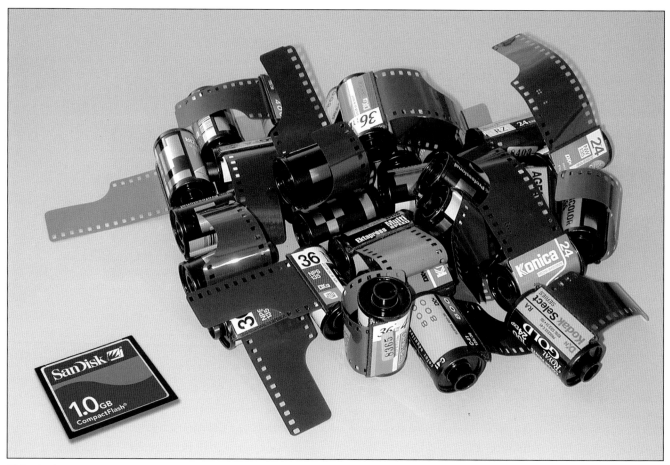

This single card can easily hold the same amount of images that could be taken with all this film.

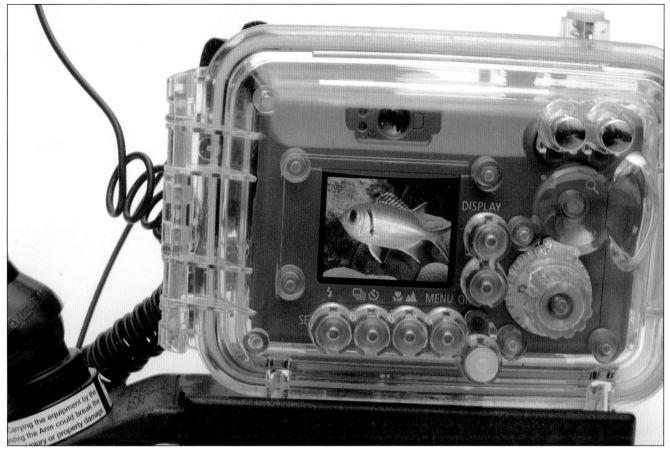

You can shoot, review, correct, and reshoot your images as you dive. Continue taking images until the image looks correct in the LCD viewer on the back of the camera.

the camera system you are considering. Below is a point-by-point comparison of film to digital, and a couple of tables that we have put together to help you make that choice. Keep in mind that this information is subjective and based on our 35-years' experience with film cameras and our use of digital cameras for 10 years.

■ FILM VS. DIGITAL

Advantages of a Digital Camera

1. Film cameras are limited to 36 exposures, while digital cameras are only limited to memory-card size and battery-power consumption. With most digital cameras, you can take over 100 images on a dive.

2. Digital cameras convert to digital files directly, while film-camera images must be scanned and digitized. The cost of a good film scanner can be over $1000, and the time required to scan the images can be five minutes per scan. Digital-camera memory cards require only the initial investment of $40 to $80, and then can be used again and again.

3. It is becoming increasingly difficult to find E-6 slide film processing. Memory cards require no processing and can be downloaded directly to your computer via a communications cable or card reader.

4. You can shoot, review, correct, and reshoot your images as you dive. You can see your image immediately and you always know if you got the shot before the dive ends. Instant gratification goes a long way towards creating enthusiasm for underwater photography. Film shooters have to wait until they process their film to know for sure. Even if they process their film during the dive trip, they risk the chance of poor processing.

5. Digital camera users don't have to worry about airport x-ray machines; neither the camera nor the memory cards will be affected. Today, airport security is increasing, and the x-ray machines are

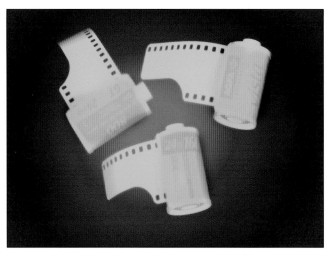

Increased security at airports makes it more difficult to fly with film systems—especially to international destinations, as x-ray machines can damage both exposed and unexposed film.

becoming more powerful. Films must be hand carried and hand checking film isn't always possible, especially with international flights.

6. Film images have a grain structure that is visible when enlarged. Digital camera images have a small amount of digital noise, but it is manageable with photo-editing software. Digital cameras can use higher ISO speeds than film cameras, which translates into greater depth of field, less required flash power, and the ability to shoot in lower light levels.

7. Digital cameras are more sensitive to available light, which, combined with higher ISO speeds, gives them an advantage on deep dives and when in low light levels.

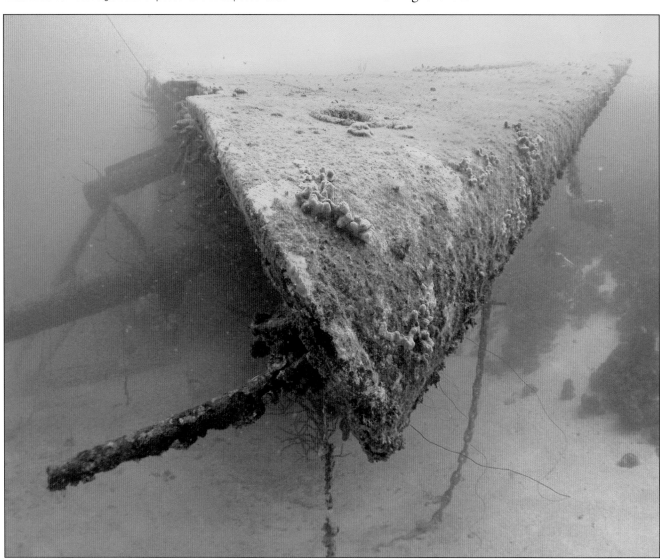

Digital cameras are more sensitive to light and can use higher ISO speeds, making it much easier to get great deep-dive images of shipwrecks.

8. The ISO speed on a digital camera can be changed from one shot to the next. Film cameras required the same ISO speed be used from image to image.

9. White balance on a digital camera allows you to bias the color of your images as you change your depth and when you switch from available light to flash.

10. Film images can easily be scratched and damaged with mishandling and environmental impact. Digital-camera files do not get scratched and can be archived directly to CD or DVD, which can last for up to 100 years.

11. Digital-camera images can be viewed directly on a television screen via a communication cable for image evaluation before the next dive.

12. Most digital cameras have either a contrast or color-saturation control that can be adjusted from one image to the next. This feature comes in handy when the subject distance from the camera and flash changes.

Advantages of a Film Camera System

1. Film cameras use much less battery power so there is less chance of a power failure during the dive. This also results in less heat buildup in the housing.

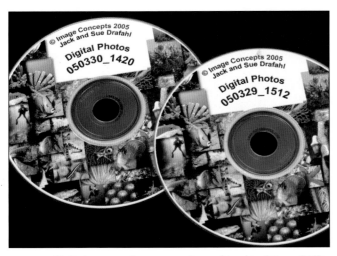

ABOVE—Digital camera images can be archived to CDs or DVDs that can last up to 100 years. We highly recommend that you make two copies of your images before you delete them from your computer or portable hard disk. RIGHT—Film shooters have an advantage when shooting into the sun. Unlike digital cameras that may have a blooming effect, film images have a smooth gradation from deep shadow to full sunlight.

2. Wide-angle images shot into the sun using a digital camera can have a blooming or posterized effect. Film camera images have a smooth, graduated tone, even when the image is overexposed.

3. High-resolution scans of fine-grain films can exceed the quality of 12-megapixel digital cameras.

4. Digital SLR cameras are prone to dust spots on the CCD and CMOS chips. Film SLR cameras rarely have problems with dust on the film plane.

5. Many film shooters have already made a large investment in cameras, lenses, and housings, and have fine-tuned their systems to achieve great results.

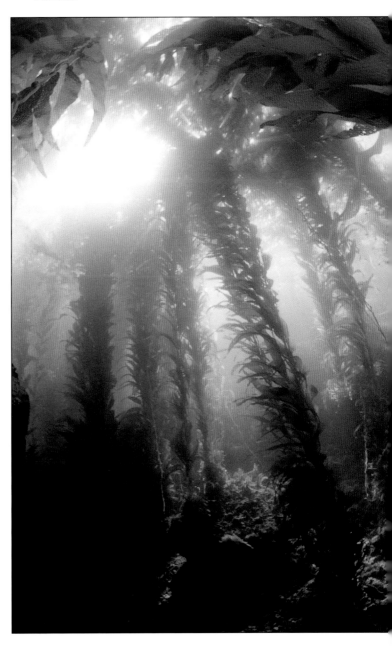

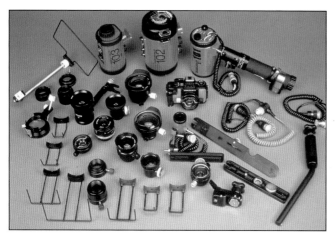
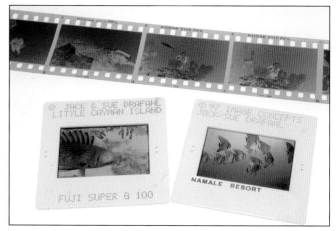

LEFT—Many underwater photographers have made a considerable investment in film systems. The camera system you see here is the Nikonos 5, one of the most popular underwater camera systems, manufactured from 1985 to 2000. RIGHT—Film images today can easily be converted to digital via film scanners. If you decide to shoot color negative film, you can even mount the negatives and scan them just as you do with slides.

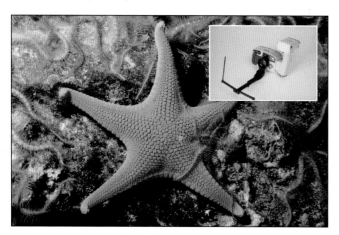
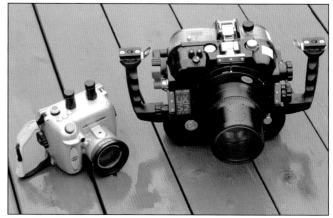

LEFT—Point & shoot film cameras are simple to use. Some even have a bayonet mount system that allows them to take both wide-angle and macro lenses. RIGHT—Compact point & shoot housings, like the one on the left, feature metal or clear polycarbonate construction and are designed to fit dozens of different camera models. Bulkier digital SLR housings, like the one on the right, use different ports to accommodate the wide variety of lenses found on the different cameras. These housings are generally made of metal and heavy-duty polycarbonate materials.

6. Color negative film still features the widest exposure latitude—up to seven stops. The most exposure latitude that any digital camera has today is about three stops. Color negative film can be processed almost anywhere in the world and can be purchased in almost every retail store.

7. With film you have the option of printing directly from the film image and then storing it safely away for later use. You can also scan the image to CD and print it as a digital image on the popular inkjet printers.

8. Film cameras are less sensitive to the heat and moisture that builds up in the housing during a dive. Sometimes digital cameras can get very hot and create a fog layer inside the housing.

9. Most film cameras are simple and easy to use. They offer very few controls which makes underwater photography decisions easy. Digital cameras can have as many as 25 different controls that require knowledge extracted from the extensive and confusing instruction manuals.

10. Film cameras can shoot sequential images faster than digital cameras. The digital camera requires more time to focus the image, shoot, and save the file.

TABLE 1—FILM VS. DIGITAL CAMERAS

You will notice that we have three film groups and only two digital groups. This is because there only one or two amphibious digital cameras on the market and they are so similar to their point & shoot siblings that we have grouped them together.

	FILM CAMERA			DIGITAL CAMERA			
	P&S	Amphibious*	SLR	3M P&S	6M P&S	6M SLR	12M SLR
4x6 prints	x	x	x	x	x	x	x
8x10 prints	x	x	x	x	x	x	x
11x14 prints	x	x	x	x	x	x	x
16x20 prints		x	x		x	x	x
Fish Portraits			x		x	x	x
Macro		x	x	x	x	x	x
Super Macro		x	x		x	x	x
Wide Angle	x	x	x	x	x	x	x
Super Wide Angle		x	x		x	x	x
Slide Shows	x	x	x	x	x	x	x
Stock		x	x		x	x	x
Magazine		x	x		x	x	x

*This group contains cameras that are self-contained and include Nikon's Nikonos camera and Sea & Sea's Motor Marine systems.

TABLE 2—DIGITAL POINT & SHOOT VS. DIGITAL SLR

POINT & SHOOT DIGITAL CAMERA	SLR DIGITAL CAMERA
Compact	Bulky
Shutter delay	No shutter delay
Lightweight for travel	Weight can cost extra for travel
Price ($200–1000)	Price ($900–5000)
LCD viewer	Optical viewfinder
Close-up function built-in	Uses macro lenses and diopters
Uses both internal and external wide-angle lenses	Internal wide-angle lens and dome port
CCD one-quarter size of film (4X more depth of field than film camera)	Depth of field same as the film camera
Zoom lens from wide angle to telephoto	Interchangeable lenses
3–8 megapixels	.6–12+ megapixels
1–2 year life span*	2–3 year life span*
Optical, cable, and slave sync**	Sync cable
Over $1/1000$ second flash sync	Limited to $1/125$ or $1/250$ second flash sync
Heat buildup due to use of internal flash (flash within the camera's underwater housing)	External flash reduces heat buildup
Clear housings more susceptible to sun's heat	Metal housings less susceptible to sun's heat
Clear acrylic housings are more fragile	Metal housings can take a beating

*The life span indicates the time the camera model is available for sale before being replaced with a newer model. Once the camera is off the market, it becomes increasingly difficult to find a replacement. This can be critical if you purchased an expensive housing specific to a particular camera model. The actual working life span of the camera will be much longer.

**There are a few point & shoot digital cameras that have an external flash-sync cable. Some are dedicated to the manufacturer's flash, while others use a standard Nikonos or Ikelite sync system.

UNDERWATER FLASH

If you are moving up from a film camera to digital, you may already have a flash unit that will work with your new digital-camera system. There are three methods for getting the camera to sync with your flash.

The oldest of the three is the sync cord that attaches directly to the camera housing and the external flash. Some units will work in TTL (through-the-lens) mode, while others only work in manual mode.

The second method is an optical cable that can be attached and reattached underwater. With this system, the internal flash is blocked so that no light emits from the front of the housing, but rather through the optical cable attached to the flash. When the internal flash fires, it triggers the external flash.

The slave triggered external flash is the third type. It can fire a flash in manual mode, or even, in some cases, when in the TTL mode.

Deciding on which flash system you require will depend on the housing you select. If you already have a flash, you need to see how it mates with the housing. If you are purchasing a flash for your housing, you should check the specifications on your camera and housing first to see that you get a flash that is totally compatible with the camera. Some digital point & shoot cameras send out a pre-flash for exposure and focus compensation; these do not synchronize with some of the older flash units. If you have this type of camera, you will need to buy a flash unit that is designed to work with pre-flash cameras. Both Ikelite (www.ikelite.com) and Sea & Sea (www.seaandsea.com) feature flash units that will work with a variety of digital cameras. You can find more information on flash photography in chapter 9.

ACCESSORY LENSES

One advantage to the digital SLR cameras is that they use film-camera lenses. It is a matter of selecting the lens you want to use and seeing if it fits in your SLR housing. If not, then you might need a new port to accommodate it.

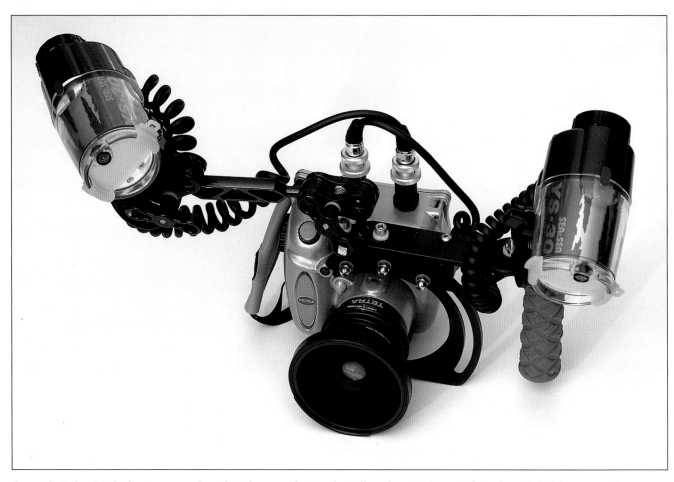

Some digital point & shoot cameras have hot shoes on the top that allow the attachment of single and double sync cords.

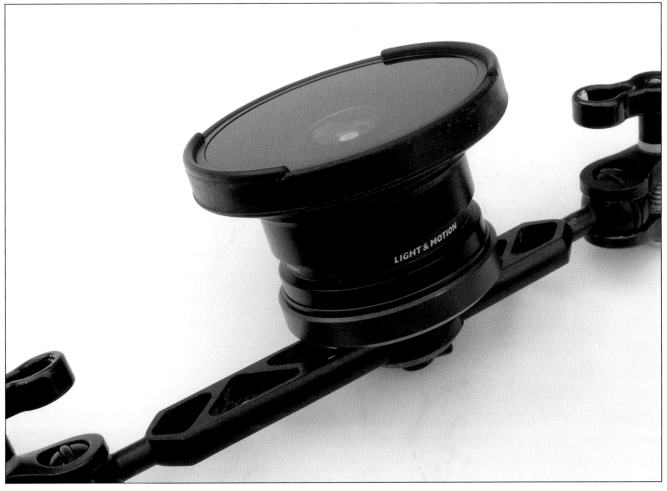

Super-wide-angle wet lenses can now be attached to the strobe arm with a thread-mounted lens caddy from INON. This allows photographers to remove the super-wide-angle lens, attach it to the lens caddy, and switch back to photograph close-ups.

To expand their focal-length capability, most all point & shoot camera housings accept auxiliary lenses. Generally, these are wide-angle wet lenses that can be attached to the camera while underwater. Larger and more expensive lenses will have threads with holes to allow the air to escape when submerged. Many of these wet lenses have 67mm threads that are interchangeable with a variety of acrylic and metal point & shoot housings. Even some of the smaller accessory lenses, like the 20mm lens for the Sea & Sea MX-10, will now bayonet onto the front of Sea & Sea's new line of digital cameras.

A couple of the point & shoot camera systems, like the Olympus 5060, have gone another direction with accessory lenses. They have added a special wide-angle port that houses a wide-angle dry lens that attaches to the front of the camera. For even more information on the use of wide-angle lenses, see chapter 10.

There are other wet accessory lenses called diopters that can fit over point & shoot housings as well as SLR housing. These specialized close-up lenses increase the magnification of many of the macro lenses to beyond 1:1. You can read more on diopters in chapter 13.

◼ FLASHLIGHTS

When you take digital cameras underwater you will quickly discover that they have difficulty focusing. This is because they rely on contrast variations to lock in the focus point, something that becomes especially critical when doing macro or close-up work. Not to worry—there is a solution. The flashlight that has been your steady companion on night dives now becomes a critical part of your digital close-up camera system. Its added light provides the clear distinction between subject and background to allow accurate focus with the digital camera.

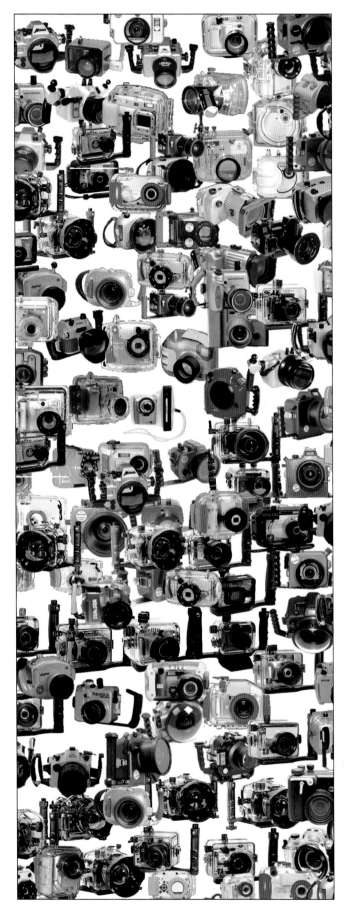

Before you buy a new flashlight, you must understand that this type of flashlight must be compact enough to fit on your camera housing, bright enough to enable the focusing system to work, and have a wide enough beam angle so that the entire image area is lit. You might consider even taking your camera and housing into the dive shop to see which one works the best. Keep in mind that a dive light that works great for night dives may work very poorly as a camera light.

■ CAMERA BRACKETS AND ARMS

In order for you to keep your whole camera system together, you will need a lightweight camera tray, arm, and bracket system. One of the best systems on the market comes from Ultralight (www.ulcs.com). It features a variety of connectors and arms designed to meet the needs of underwater photographers. The exact configuration you select will depend on what type of photography you intend on doing. You will need a compact tray and short arms for macro work so that the flash units are close to the lens. When trying wide angle photography, you need to use the strobe or strobes extended out on long arms to keep them away from the camera for even lighting and to minimize backscatter.

With add-on systems from Ultralight, you can insert arm extensions to achieve long flash distances, or adapters that support two connections so you can add a flashlight and strobe. If your camera system is heavy, there are even floater arms that have air pockets to provide that added lift.

If you like shooting both horizontal and vertical images, you should consider a camera tray that allows quick camera rotation. In addition to rotating the camera 90 degrees, it keeps the flash in the same position for both images. This system really reduces the need to reposition the flash every time you change camera angles.

There are other manufacturers that provide even more handy tools for the underwater photographer. One we specifically like is a lens caddy from INON

By 2005, more than 700 digital cameras were on the market, and new models were coming out weekly. Underwater housings had already surpassed the 300 mark, although many manufacturers supported the same camera model.

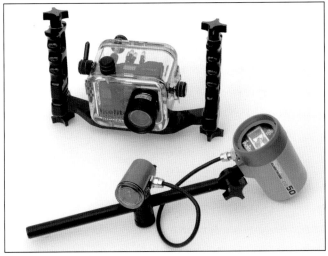

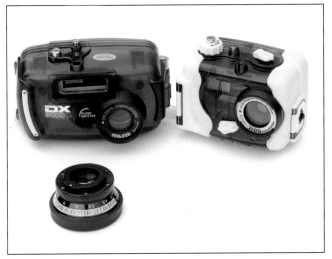

LEFT—Ikelite has the largest selection of both SLR and point & shoot underwater housings. They also make electronic flash units and TTL slave sensors that interface with other point & shoot underwater housings. RIGHT—Sea & Sea has made the transition from film to digital by incorporating its bayonet wet lens design in its digital camera line. The same lenses that fit on the MX-10 now fit on cameras like the DX-3000 and the amphibious AquaPix.

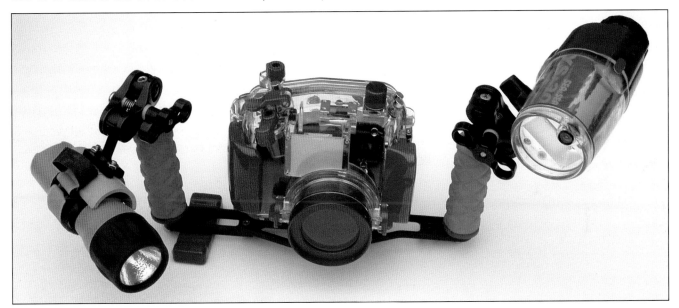

Many of the camera manufacturers, like Olympus, have jumped into the market offering compact housings that adapt to a variety of underwater flash configurations. The housing here is mounted on the universal Ultralight camera tray with its twin handles designed to handle flash or flashlight.

(www.inonamerica.com). It attaches to the side of the arms to allow you a safe place to store your wet wide-angle lens when it is not in use. Although many of the arm and bracket systems can be intermixed, we have found that it is best to stick with one brand throughout your entire camera system to assure compatibility.

■ FACE MASK

You would not think that a face mask would be considered part of your photo gear, but when it comes to dig-ital cameras, your face mask is critical. Film cameras only had control knobs and levers to adjust underwater, but the digital camera brings with it a new set of visual problems. The LCD menus and control knob labels are difficult to see on digital-camera underwater housings. The LCD menus are either too small for the unaided eye to see or the control-knob lettering seems to blend in with its surroundings. The problem is that all this information is needed to achieve accurate focus and exposure.

So what's the solution? Since this camera information is vital, you will want to consider adding a diopter inside your mask, even if you don't normally wear glasses. It will just provide that added magnification to help you discern the digital data. The two types of diopters will either fill the entire viewing area, or just a small area at the bottom of the mask, much like bifocal glasses. The one you decide to use is a personal preference. Most dive shops have face-mask diopters in stock, or they can be special ordered. There are also several companies that specialize in prescription face masks, so check with your local dive shop for availability.

> Most dive shops have face-mask diopters in stock, or they can be special ordered.

We both like to use a fully corrected lens in one side of the mask and none in the other side. This way we can read very small text with one eye and still see distant objects with the other. It seems like this configuration might be confusing, but surprisingly the brain will combine the two views so that you see everything in focus from just a few inches away to infinity. It is a bit disorienting on the first dive, but the human brain can quickly adjust to this visual configuration. The magnification should be strong enough so that you can clearly read the smallest lettering on the LCD view finder. This type of mask also has the added advantage that you can now see some really tiny creatures as you cruise the reefs.

■ WEB HELP

Bet you thought buying an underwater camera system would be easy, right? We realize that this is a lot of information to digest, but hopefully you will only have to refer to it once every few years as you expand your underwater photographic skills and need to upgrade your camera system.

One question that everyone asks is which should you buy first, the camera or housing? When digital underwater first began, the answer was simple, since there were only a few housings in existence. Today, it is not uncommon for several of the manufacturers to offer housings almost simultaneously with a new camera's announcement.

The best place to start your equipment search is on the Web. We recommend that you find a couple of digital cameras that meet your needs, and then start a search to find the best housing choices. If there is no housing available for your first camera choice, then maybe try your alternate selection. You might also contact a custom housing manufacturer like Ikelite (www.ikelite.com) to see if they can create a custom housing for the camera you have selected.

Two of the best Web pages we have found to start your research are www.wetpixel.com and www.digideep.com. Wetpixel features new product reviews, tutorials, and Web links to all the digital camera and housing manufacturers. Using these links you can go to specific manufacturers' pages to see if their housing-and-camera combinations fit your specific needs. The folks at Digideep make it their full-time job to maintain an updated list showing all the underwater housing-and-camera combinations that are currently available.

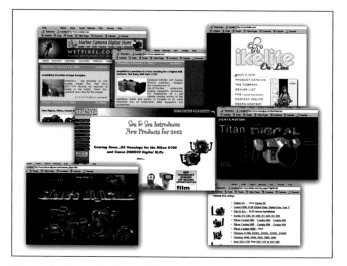

Research for matching digital cameras and housings is best done on the Web. You can either go to the camera and housing manufacturer's page, or to specially designed resource pages like www.digideep.com and www.wetpixel.com.

4. Digital-Camera Components

The digital camera is a very complex photographic instrument and can overwhelm even the most educated person. Dozens of buttons and controls, not to mention the lengthy instruction manuals, are enough to make you lose sight of the fact that your original objective was just to take a picture. We felt it was necessary to include a chapter that laid out all the basic components of a digital camera, so that you would have something to refer to when we discussed a specific camera control. What makes it a bit easier is that there are only two types of digital cameras: point & shoot and SLR. If you're unsure of the basic differences between the two, you can look back at table 2 in chapter 3 (page 17).

■ CAMERA PARTS

When you look at the fronts of digital cameras, they look much like their film counterparts. The point & shoot cameras have a zoom lens, sensor for focus and exposure, and an optical viewfinder. Many have a pop-

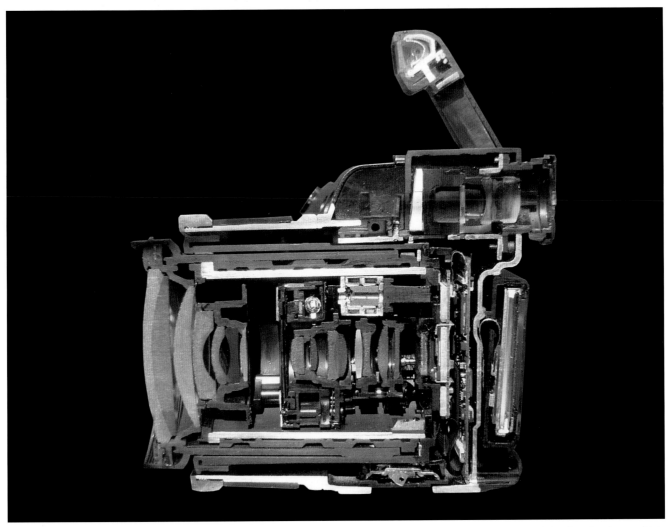

As you can see from this cut-away view of an Olympus 8-megapixel model, these cameras are packed full of technology, which makes them more fragile than film cameras.

up or built-in flash on the front, much like the film versions. The front of the digital SLR camera is so much like its film counterpart that it is often difficult to tell whether it's digital or film. The interchangeable lens mount, hot shoe, exposure-mode controls, focus controls, depth of field, f/stop, and focus ring are almost identical. The top of the digital point & shoot and SLR cameras, again, are almost the same as the film versions. The LCD (liquid crystal display) menu displays for shutter speed, f/stop, flash control, and battery power are all similar, too.

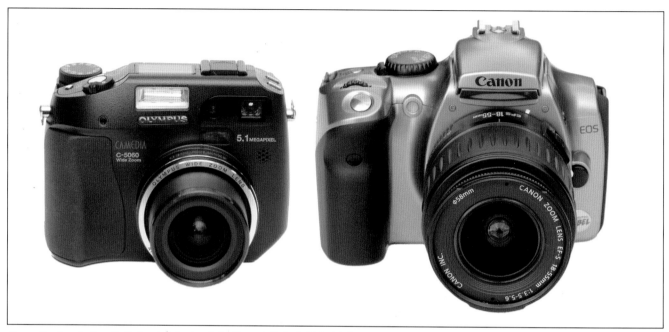

From the front, the digital point & shoot (left) and digital SLR (right) cameras look much like their film counterparts. The point & shoot will have a zoom lens, flash, and viewfinder, while the SLR features an ergonomic grip, interchangeable lenses, and the prism viewfinder.

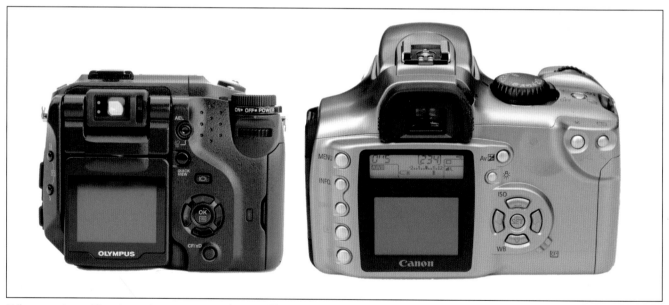

When you turn either type of camera around, you will instantly see the difference; an LCD viewer, control panel, and various buttons are used to control a wide variety of digital camera functions. The point & shoot camera (left) will use the viewfinder at the top and/or the LCD viewer at the bottom for composing and shooting the image. Most underwater housings block the top viewfinder, so you exclusively use the LCD viewer underwater. The SLR camera uses the optical viewer at the top for composing and taking the image. The results are then previewed on the LCD viewer at the bottom.

◼ LCD DISPLAY

It's not until you turn the camera around that the real difference between digital and film cameras becomes obvious.

On digitals, the LCD display on the back of the camera allows you to view, compose, and review your images from a distance. With the point & shoot digital cameras, the LCD is also used to adjust many of the camera menus. The SLR digital camera utilizes the LCD monitor to review the image and adjust the camera menus, but generally the SLR cameras still use the optical viewfinder system at the top of the camera for framing and focus.

Some the LCD displays are permanently mounted on the back of the camera while others can be twisted and rotated so that you can preview and shoot pictures from unusual angles. In almost all cases though, the LCD viewer is kept in the flat position when installed in an underwater housing.

◼ BUTTON, BUTTONS, AND MORE BUTTONS

The most overwhelming part of a digital camera is all the buttons surrounding the LCD viewer on the back of the camera. There can be more than a dozen controls whose purpose will be quickly forgotten as soon as you go underwater. Some of the possible buttons are for focus lock, exposure lock, exposure compensation, ISO speed, exposure bracketing, close-up mode, flash control, self-timer, monitor off/on, trash, sharpness, image compression, image resolution, preview, camera setup, and more.

The menu system is accessed via one of these button controls, and from there you can toggle settings by pressing left, right, up, or down to maneuver through the menu. The good news is that most of these buttons are not needed for use underwater. Once you learn how to turn the camera on, frame the subject, and press the shutter, you are headed in the right direction toward getting some great underwater images.

The biggest problem you will encounter will be concerning exposure, so we devote an entire chapter to it, beginning on page 46. Once you get your exposure systems down, the rest is a matter of learning one or two controls per day of diving until you finally master the entire system. The key is not to read the entire man-

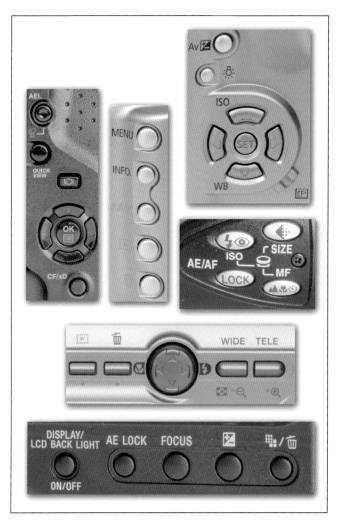

All of these buttons can be confusing and frustrating. Once you master them, though, you will quickly realize the control they provide in your underwater photography.

ual trying to learn the whole camera at once. You will find it exacerbating—it may even lead you to thoughts of hocking your entire digital camera system! You should try to learn the camera's defaults at first and then work up to each control one at a time.

◼ CHIP COMPONENT

The inside of the camera is where all the electronic magic occurs. It is composed of optics, electronics, firmware, and an image-recording device. The optics are what make up the zoom-lens and focusing system, which delivers an inverted image to the inside back of the camera. This image is recorded by an electronic light-sensitive device called a CCD (Charged Coupled Device) or CMOS (Charged Metal Oxide Sensor). Both of these systems are controlled with a software and

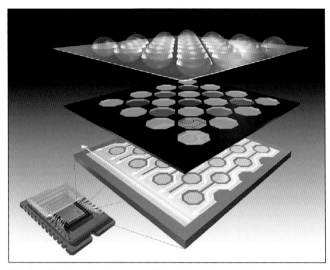

During the few short years of digital photography, more than a dozen different image-sensor designs have increased resolution and exposure latitude. These sensors may be positioned in rows and columns, diagonals, or even stacked in layers for maximum capability. (Image courtesy of Fuji Photo.)

hardware combination called firmware. This is what controls the communication between the buttons you push on the outside and the automated systems inside the camera.

◼ BATTERIES

Digital cameras require a lot of power to run the LCD monitor, focus controls, and image-capture system. For that reason most all digital cameras use either Lithium Ion or Ni-MH (Nickel Metal Hydride) rechargeable batteries which are designed to deliver an enormous amount of power. If you use Ni-MH batteries, we recommend at least 1800mhh to ensure that the camera will not completely run out of power before the dive ends.

With digital you are not restricted to 36 exposures per dive. This is a great feature, but it can also cause some problems. If you rapidly take pictures or shoot over 200 images on a dive, it can cause the camera housing to overheat. We recommend trying to keep the number of images below 150 so that you don't overheat and potentially damage the system. Remember that underwater camera housings have no way to vent the heat they create until you open the housing at the end of the dive.

When traveling with your digital camera, be sure to have plenty of batteries. That way you can always have a set charging. Be sure to mark each set of batteries so that different types of batteries or power ratings are not mixed together. If a battery with a low milliamp rating is mixed in with higher rated batteries, it will force the higher values down to the lower ones during the charge. One of the best ways to check and see if your batteries are charged is to use a battery-load tester; we have found a great one from Ultralight.

If you plan international dive travel and you use Ni-MH batteries, you will want to pick up an international charger that is rated for 100–240 volts and 50/60

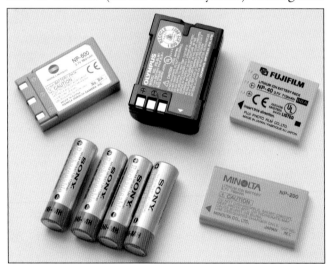

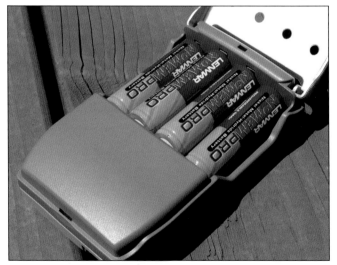

LEFT—Digital camera batteries today basically come in two types. The Ni-MH batteries (lower left) are generally AA, while the proprietary Lithium Ion batteries come in all shapes and sizes. Both types work well and provide effective digital-camera operation. RIGHT—For international travel, purchase a 50/60 cycle, 120–240 volt charger; U.S. versions may overheat and burn out when operated on international systems.

cycle. If you try to use a 120-volt, 60-cycle charger on a different electrical system, the charger will overhead and burn out.

■ MEMORY CARDS

Memory cards are used for storing digital-camera files and are inserted into slots found on the back, side, or bottom of the digital camera. Some cameras even have slots to accept two different types of cards. Memory cards can only be inserted one way into the camera, so if the card doesn't fit, don't force it. Look closely at the card or the slot; there should be instructions on its insertion. If you have trouble, you may have to consult the instruction manual for help.

There are many sizes of memory cards available on the market, and the incorrect assumption by new digital photographers is they should get the largest they can afford. After extensive testing and interviews with other digital photographers, we suggest that 128–256 megabyte (MB) cards work well for 3–6 megapixel cameras, and 256–512MB cards are a good choice for 6–12 megapixel cameras.

In both cases, you can shoot one or two dives before the card is full. Since you almost always need to change batteries on every dive, you might as well do the same with the memory cards. That way, you are not putting all your eggs into one electronic basket. We also recommend that you should have enough memory cards to go the entire dive day without having to stop and transfer off the images from the cards. That way when the day is done, you can leisurely transfer your images and prepare for the next day of diving.

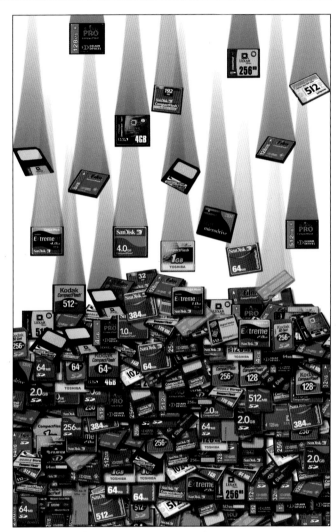

There are more than 12 different types of memory cards on the market today that range from 8MB to 8 gigabytes (GB). Since there are dozens of manufacturers, this means there are more memory-card configurations than film types on the market today.

5. Digital-Camera Menu Controls

The most frustrating aspect of digital photography is the menu systems. They can be very complicated and can often take you deep into the submenu dungeons where you seem to travel endlessly. The advantage to all your delving efforts is that these menus provide an enormous amount of control over your digital camera. So, you have a choice: you can look at these menu options as too many controls to learn because you're frustrated, or you can regard them as a very powerful tool that is just waiting for a test dive. We'll assume that you are up for a challenge, so we'll try and help you make sense of the menus.

■ DEFAULT IS GOOD
When you first start taking pictures with your digital camera, we recommend that you leave all the menu settings on the factory default. The camera company has spent lots of time determining the best settings for general photography, so their defaults will work fine until you learn how to modify each menu control.

We find that the best method for learning the controls is to work specifically with one or two controls at a time. This may require that you read about these controls in your instruction manual, but don't panic—you won't have to read the entire manual at once! Menu controls vary from camera to camera, so if you can't find a menu control discussed below, the control is either hidden or possibly not available on your specific camera model.

Our number-one rule with a new digital camera is that you need to be able to locate and operate the different controls with your eyes closed. When you feel confident, then put the camera in the housing and try it again. You need to be extremely comfortable with locating all the buttons and menu choices before you ever jump overboard. As divers, we all know that as we descend, our brain has plenty of other concerns beyond camera operation.

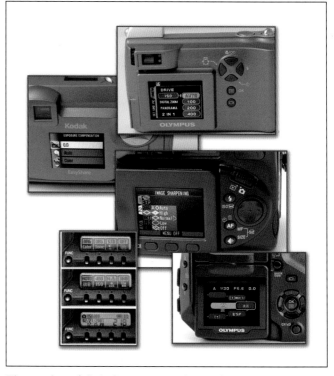

The number of digital cameras on the market can be somewhat overwhelming. Keep in mind that most of the control menus are set to defaults when you start, which is a big help when you take these electronic marvels underwater.

■ WHITE BALANCE
The white-balance function is used to bias the color-temperature setting of your image sensor to compensate for the color temperature of different light sources. This is one of the most powerful controls on a digital camera and one of the biggest differences between film and digital cameras. To achieve the same balance, film users have to use color-correction filters or color films especially designed to match these color-temperature situations.

The default white-balance setting in a digital camera is auto. This means that as the camera shoots the picture, it looks for a white, black, and a midtone value, then tries to balance the color as best as possible. This works great topside, but underwater it can cause prob-

When shooting macro images with flash, the best settings for most digital cameras are the flash or sunlight settings. Try both on the same subject at the beginning of a dive so that you can record the world of the small with the best color balance.

lems. If you were to take an available-light image consisting mainly of blue water and blue sky, the camera might end up creating an image with posterized red highlights or shadows. When you shoot a close-up image of a red starfish on a red sponge using the auto white-balance setting, you will probably end up with a gray image very lacking in color. For that reason, white balance is the first control that you will want to adjust from the default.

The choices for white balance will vary from camera to camera. Almost all will have daylight, tungsten, fluorescent, flash, cloudy, and custom settings. Some of the more advanced cameras will also have a shade setting, or multiple versions of the custom and fluorescent white-balance settings.

Your first change to the white balance setting will be determined by the lighting method in the scene. If you are shooting your underwater images with available light, the scene will usually be blue, so you can use the sunlight setting if you want little change in the color. If, on the other hand, you want the colors to be warmer and reduce the blue, try the cloudy setting. If you want to make it even warmer, use the shade setting (if it is available with your camera). If you are diving in greener waters like, Cayman Island's Stingray City, Santa Barbara Channel Islands, or even on deep wrecks, you can try the fluorescent white-balance setting. The fluorescent setting is designed to remove the green cast given off by fluorescent lights, so it works similarly with green water. If you don't like the results produced by the fluorescent white-balance setting, then try the cloudy or shade setting.

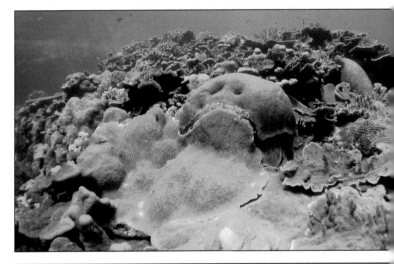

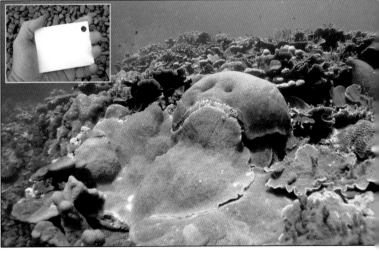

ABOVE—The white-balance is one of the most powerful digital-camera menu controls. Most digital cameras have several presets as well as a custom preset that you can set yourself. TOP RIGHT—This image, taken in the Solomon Islands, shows the results of using the auto white-balance setting. TOP LEFT—This time we metered a white card to create a custom white balance, then used that setting to bias the color balance in the scene.

The custom white balance is an advanced color control that can prove to be a very powerful tool. When you set your digital camera to custom white balance, you will be asked to take a sample reading of an area that is supposedly white. This is done by pressing a menu button or the shutter. Don't worry—the camera's menu system will tell you which one to push and when. The problem is that you would assume that white sand or dead coral would provide a good white balance, but you'd be wrong. We have tried many times, and in most all cases, the custom white balance has a red bias.

The best solution is to carry a small white piece of white plastic or a slate in your BC (buoyancy compensator) pocket and point the camera at it for measuring the white balance. Keep in mind that the color temperature of the underwater scene changes for every foot that you descend. To get an accurate white balance, you must measure it at the same depth you'll be shooting at. You can use this to your advantage. For example, if you want to warm up a scene at a depth of 10 feet, go down to 15 or 20 feet, take your white balance setting, save it, then come back up to 10 feet and use that setting. The results will be a warmer image than you would have gotten using the white balance taken at 10 feet. Some of the more advanced digital cameras have multiple white balance settings so you can make one at 10, 20, and 30 feet. Then you can pick and choose your setting to match the desired color balance.

We have also seen some of the newer digital cameras with a visual custom white balance. With this setting, you simply turn a control knob until you can see the color balance you want in the LCD viewer. Save it and you are in business. Isn't technology great?

■ ISO SPEEDS

Unlike film cameras, you can adjust the ISO of a digital camera from image to image. It's easy to change the ISO sensitivity of the CCD or CMOS chip with a simple press of a button. We have seen digital cameras with an ISO settings as low as 50 and as high as 6400, but most range from ISO 100–800.

Film shooters entering the digital world tend to use the lowest ISO speed possible with the thoughts of minimizing the grain pattern. Digital cameras do not have grain, but do have a similar effect called digital noise. This noise is considerably less of a problem than film grain, so you can use the higher ISO speeds without worrying about quality degradation.

We recommend the use of ISO 100–200 for macro or close-up images, ISO 200–400 for reef scenes and fish photography, and ISO 400–800 for distant subjects and available-light images. A big advantage of the higher ISO speeds is the potential for increased depth of field by using smaller f/stops. You can also use smaller flash units that require less power. These units provide shorter flash durations in the TTL mode, so flash recycle times are reduced. Available-light photography using higher ISO speeds also allows for the use of higher shutter speeds to stop movement and provide sharper images.

If the concept of using the higher ISO speeds still bothers you, you should also know that a company

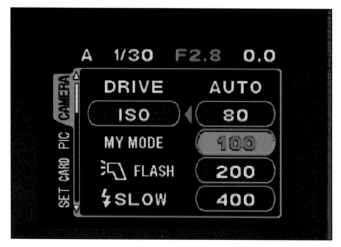

Another advantage with digital cameras is the ability to change the ISO from image to image. This can be done using menus or control buttons found on the back or top of the camera.

WHITE BALANCE BELOW 30 FEET

We don't recommend taking an available-light white-balance reading below 30 feet. Most camera systems will bias the color too much below this depth and provide posterized colors. If you want to use your custom white balance settings at greater depths, just take a reading at 30 feet, save it, and then use that same setting at the lower depths.

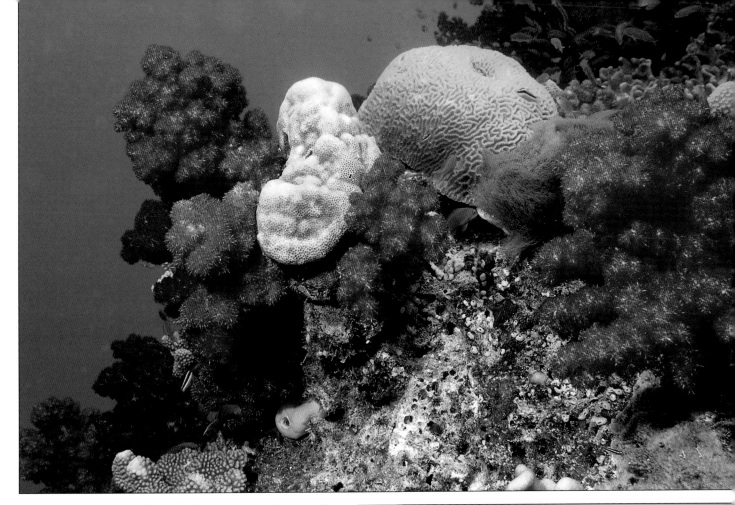

ABOVE—Digital cameras have much less noise (grain) than film cameras, so you can easily shoot at higher ISO speeds when the light level drops. RIGHT—You can use ISO 400–800 to ensure that you have a high enough shutter speed to stop the action and still maintain adequate depth of field.

called nik Multimedia (www.nikmultimedia.com) has created an Adobe Photoshop plug-in program called Dfine that can dramatically reduce digital camera noise. This program can be applied to the entire image or just specific colors and sections of the image. The bottom line is that with digital if you need the ISO speed, it's okay to use it.

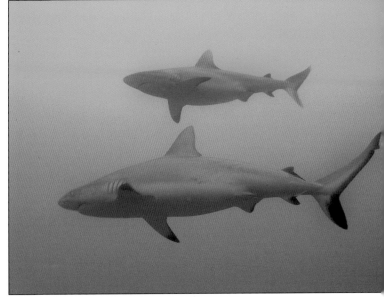

■ FLASH

The flash controls for a digital camera are usually adjusted using a button located on the back of the camera. Simply press this button and it cycles you through the various types of flash settings until you find the one you want. The default is auto, which means that the camera looks at the light level in the scene and will turn the flash on when needed. If you see a lighting bolt on the screen, this mean the flash will fire every time, no matter what the light level. Most underwater camera systems will use this setting. The lighting bolt with a line through it means the flash is turned off. This is the setting you would use for available light.

The eyeball icon represents the red-eye reduction setting, which is not much use underwater—unless the squirrel fish you are photographing gets a red-eye

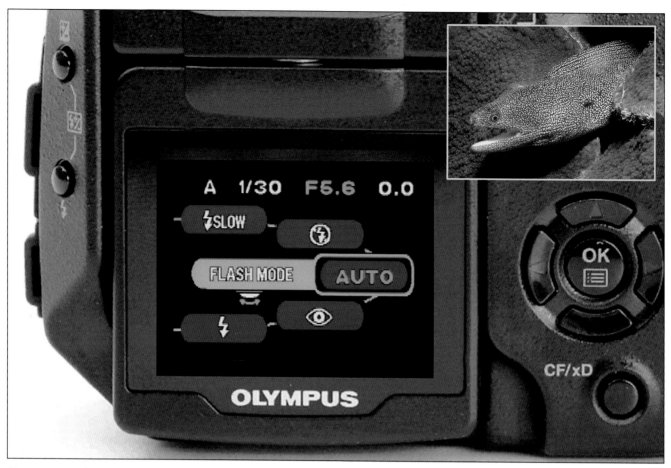

Most cameras have auto, flash on, flash off, red-eye reduction, and slow flash sync.

reflection (just kidding!). The slow flash icon is usually represented with a night scene, and forces the camera to fire the flash at a correct exposure while balancing the available light. This setting is a great creative effect that you can use for creating ghosted images where both blurred and sharp subjects move through a scene. Again, this is function that serves more purpose above water than below.

■ SHARPNESS

The factory default setting for sharpness is usually auto. This means that the sharpness varies from shot to shot, depending on the detail contained in an image. Generally this is acceptable, but not with every scene. If you are shooting an available-light image, leaving the sharpness set on auto may cause the digital noise to be unacceptable. Check your camera to see if there is a normal setting, and if so, reset it to that.

The sharpness control should be set in proportion to the water column between the camera and the sub-ject. If most of your subjects are very close to the camera, then you would set the sharpness to normal or less than normal. If the subject is quite some distance from the camera, you would set the sharpness to normal or higher than normal.

To really see how much the sharpness setting affects your images, we highly recommend that you photograph a single subject using all the sharpness settings, including no sharpening. Bring them all into your editing program and sharpen the image that you took without any camera sharpening using the editing software. Use the zoom tool and enlarge the image and compare it with similar areas in the images that were sharpened in the camera. Make sure you try this procedure with close-ups, normal shots, and wide-angle images to make a fair evaluation.

■ CONTRAST

The default for this menu setting will also be auto, which means that the contrast will vary from shot to shot depending on the lighting and subject matter. The best overall setting for consistant shooting would be normal. If you find the water visibility low, such as while on a wreck, you may want to bump up the contrast to enhance the diffused shapes in the scene.

If you are taking images into the sun using a wide-angle lens, you may see a blooming effect where the colors are not distinct, especially in the bright areas. This is caused by the image sensor's inability to define highlight detail from the bright area to the surrounding areas. This posterized effect can be reduced by adjusting the contrast to its lowest setting. Make sure you set it back when you return to shooting images without the sun in the picture.

◼ SATURATION

Again, the default for most digital cameras is going to be auto, which means that you should change it to nor-

mal to maintain consistency from one image to the next. The saturation control is handy when shooting with digital SLRs and long macro lenses. For example, when shooting with a 60mm macro, you would use the normal setting for the best color saturation. The 105mm macro doubles the water column between the lens and the subject, thus reducing the subject's contrast and color saturation. In this case, set the saturation control to a higher level to compensate.

If you are shooting into the sun and have the blooming effect we mentioned previously, you will find that lowering the saturation level below the normal setting will also help reduce the blooming effect.

◼ EXPOSURE

Exposure Compensation. Exposure compensation control comes in three flavors. The more basic digital cameras will have one exposure control that will bias the

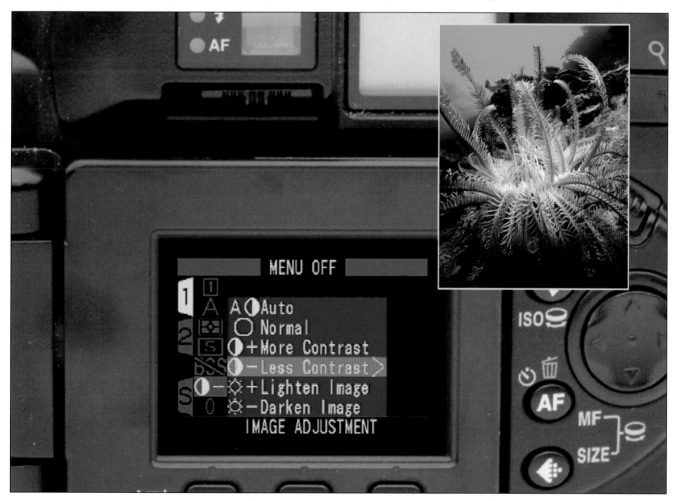

More digital cameras today have controls for adjusting contrast and/or color saturation. If you find the scene lighting too extreme, you can decrease these settings and capture a wider exposure range.

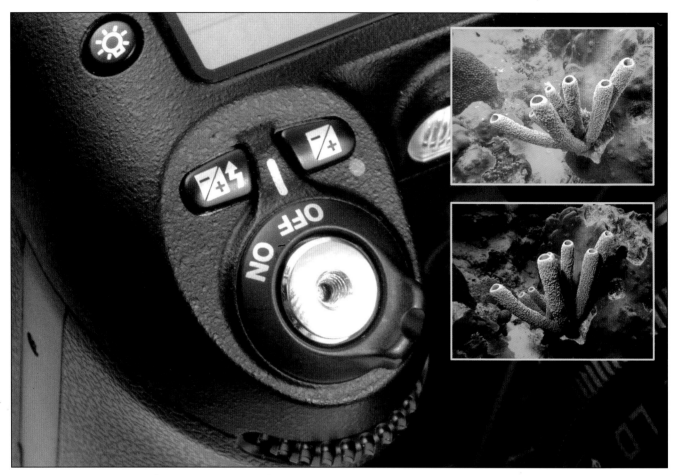

Exposure compensation on digital cameras varies from image exposure compensation to separate controls for available light and flash. This digital SLR camera has one for flash compensation (left), and another button to adjust the available light (right). The key is to keep adjusting them until you see the desired results in the LCD viewer on the back of the camera.

overall exposure of both available light and flash. If your images tend to be overexposed or light, use the minus setting. If your exposures are dark or underexposed most of time, then use the plus setting. On some cameras, the exposure-compensation setting only affects the available-light settings. If you're not sure which your camera controls, check the manual or run a test with both flash and available light to see which it affects.

The more advanced digital cameras will have a separate setting for available light and flash. Adjusting each with a plus or minus setting will only regulate the light source you have selected. This is a very helpful function when you are trying to balance the foreground that is lit by flash with the available-light background. You will find more information about this function in chapter 7 on obtaining good exposures.

Point & shoot cameras that have a hot shoe or external flash-sync port will have a flash-control menu that allows you to fire either the internal and external flash, or just the external flash. Some of the more advanced point & shoot camera models may even have a slave function designed to activate external slaved flash units.

Exposure Bracket. The exposure-bracket feature automatically sets your camera to take an overexposure, a normal image, and one underexposure as soon as you press the shutter. For those digital cameras with enough on-board memory to shoot continuous images in available light, one press of the shutter will take all three images. Otherwise, you must press the shutter three times in order to accomplish the exposure cycle. In most digital cameras, if you have the flash turned on, you must press the shutter three times to get all three exposures. You will also have to wait long enough for the flash to cycle between shots. Consult your manual to see how your camera addresses this function.

One unusual feature we have seen listed under the bracket setting is a specialized white-balance bracket. With this function set, the camera will take one image with normal white balance, one with a cooler balance, and one warmer. You can adjust the presets for this control so you achieve only a slight color change or a drastic alteration.

■ FOCUSING

Focus Brackets. The focus brackets are a special control that, when in auto, allows the camera to decide the most critical point of focus. Usually it is set to focus in the center of the image, but that isn't always where the animal you are photographing decides to settle. If you set the focus brackets to manual control, the camera doesn't go into manual focus, but rather allows you to use the menu toggle to adjust the focus point. For example, imagine you want to focus on a fish's eye and the fish is located to the left of the center point of the image. Simply use the toggle to move the focus brackets to the left side of the image and your fish's eye will be in focus. This is also a great function when taking vertical wide-angle photos where the small subject is at the bottom of the image. Stay tuned, as there will be more on this technique in chapter 10.

Continuous Focus. When the camera is set to continuous focus, this means that the camera system is always looking for a focus point, no matter where it is pointed. As you swim along with the camera pointed down, it will focus on what it sees and it will continue searching until it locks on a subject. The advantage to this function is that the focus is fast, and the shutter delay is considerably reduced. The downside is that the battery runs down faster, and there is more wear and tear on your camera as it is constantly focusing.

Close-Up Mode. The flower symbol is one of the icons found on every point & shoot digital camera made today. This signifies the close-up mode, where the

TOP—The default mode will generally have the focus point located in the center of the image. If you photograph objects close to the camera lens, part of the subject may be out of focus. BOTTOM—Move the focus point up/down, or left/right so that the depth of field position best suits your subject's focus position.

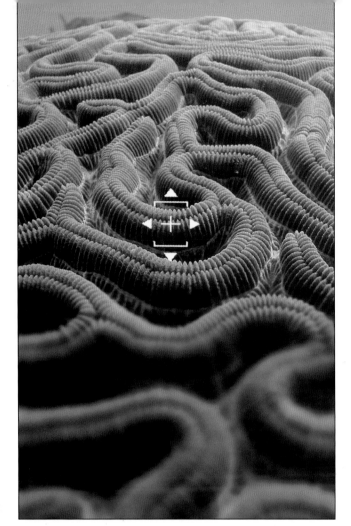
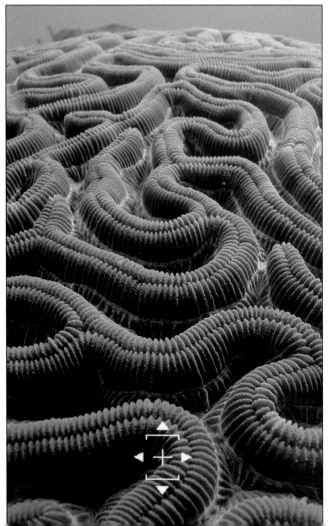

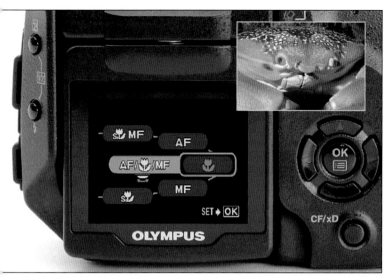

The one feature that closes the gap between point & shoot cameras and the digital SLR is its ability to shoot close-ups (flower icon). Some cameras even include manual focus, and super macro modes to get you in even closer.

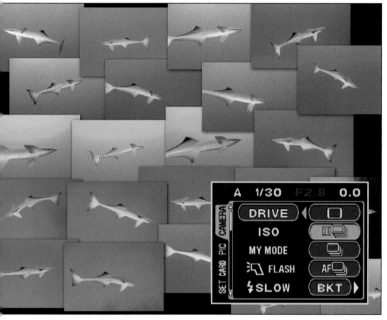

There are dozens of continuous-shooting drive modes found on both point & shoot and digital SLR cameras. These settings allow you to shoot a continuous series of images in a very short time. At the end of the sequence, you generally have to wait a few seconds as the camera transfers the group of images to your memory card.

camera forces the lens elements to adjust for closer focusing.

With some cameras, you will notice that the lens jumps to the wide angle position when the close-up mode is selected. If your camera does this, you will not be able to use the zoom function while in the close-up

mode. To get the subject larger in the viewfinder, you will have to move the camera lens closer to the subject.

If your camera does not change focal lengths when you press the close-up button, this usually means that you can use the zoom function to enlarge your close-up subject. Sometimes, you may still find that your camera doesn't function while in the close-up mode if you use the zoom function. You may need to back off from full zoom or turn the close-up function off and then back on and refrain from using the zoom function.

When in doubt as to what limitations you might have with your close-up function, refer to the trusty instruction manual.

Super Macro Mode. We are now starting to see cameras featuring a super macro function. This is essentially a close-up function that sets the lens to a higher magnification and allows you to get even closer to your subject. Generally speaking, there will be two controls with this function: auto focus and manual. Since the focus is very critical, the auto-focus function isn't always the best choice. You will find that using the manual focus and moving the camera back and forth slightly will allow you to capture the best focus point. Many of these cameras can now capture subjects at the 1:1 and 2:1 magnification levels.

■ CONTINUOUS-SHOOTING MODE

There many variations of this mode and the one you have will depend on the manufacturer and model of camera you are using. The resolution and number of images the camera can capture depends on the amount of on-board camera memory. Among the higher-end models, we have seen cameras that can shoot five high resolution images in a row. Another can shoot 25 in a row—but only saves out the best five. Some of the lower-resolution cameras have the ability to shoot from 10 to 30 medium-resolution images a second for a length of one or two minutes before saving the image group. There are even some digital cameras that can shoot 9 to 16 very low-resolution images in a row and create one composite image from the group.

If you like shooting time-lapse video, there is a menu function on a few cameras that shoots in the intervalometer mode. With this mode, the camera takes images at preset intervals until the camera battery is dead or the memory card is full. The still images can be placed on a timeline and saved as a time-lapse video. This is the function you would use to shoot a video of a starfish slowly moving across the ocean bottom.

RESOLUTION

Most digital cameras feature several image resolutions that range from high quality to Internet quality. As the resolution goes down, you can save more images on each memory card. However, this limits your options later. For example, if you *do* shoot at a lower resolution, you may eventually decide you want to enlarge one of your great images, only to discover the image quality is not satisfactory for making a large print. For this reason alone, it makes sense to shoot all your images at the highest resolution your camera features. Should you need a lower resolution version for the Internet, just reduce it later in your image-editing program. If you find yourself needing to shoot at a lower resolution just so you can get more images on a memory card, you simply need to buy a larger memory card—or two!

FILE COMPRESSION

This is a hotly debated topic. Most professioanls will tell you to shoot in the RAW format to get the best quality and that JPEG compression is too low in quality.

We partially disagree with the majority. The increased range of the RAW file far exceeds the image qualities of the JPEG format, especially in available light situations. We now recommend that DSLR shooters use RAW for everything they shoot underwater. While most DSLRs can shoot both RAW and JPEG simultaneously, we don't recommend it. The extra JPEG file can confuse the situation when using the Camera RAW editor in Adobe Photoshop, and you can always create a JPEG copy later. The RAW format makes no contrast, saturation, sharpness, or color balance adjustments to your image so you must do all that in your editing program.

It is a different story when using point & shoot cameras. When you select the RAW mode, it can take your camera as long as 15 seconds to download the RAW file each time you take a shot. By the time you are ready for the next shot, the fish is gone—and you only have room for a few more shots on your memory card. In this case, consider shooting JPEG for scenes that are illuminated by flash and RAW for available light. Another advantage is JPEG comes partially corrected into your editing program.

Although some of the newer point & shoot cameras have the ability to shoot both RAW and JPEG, we don't recommend it.

After extensive testing, we have found no visible difference between the quality of RAW and JPEG formats when correctly exposed, except in available light. We feel the JPEG format, saved at the highest quality setting, is a good choice because of its short capture time, minimal storage space on your memory card, and image quality. Don't just take our word for it; make your own comparisons and judge for yourself.

ACCESSORY LENSES

Many of the more advanced point & shoot digital cameras have filter threads on the front of the zoom lens that allow you to add accessory lenses. The lens menu will display a list of possible telephoto and wide-angle lenses that can be added to your camera. If you use a fisheye lens, the menu will also have options for either circle or full-frame fisheye. When you attach the accessory lens and make your lens selection from the lens menu, the camera will adjust the primary lens to the optimum focal length for that accessory lens.

SOUND RECORD

The sound-record feature comes in two variations. When activated with a menu control, the first type will allow you to add a small audio memo clip as you shoot still images. The recording time restriction varies between camera models (some will allow you to adjust the time length). The second type of sound recording allows you to add sound to any image after it has been taken. You simply go to the image preview and activate the sound record. You can then speak into the camera or add music to each still image. Again the recording length varies, but most cameras have a longer record time with this function than with the memo type.

EXIF HISTOGRAM PLAYBACK

Digital cameras store shooting data called EXIF metadata with each file. If you want to analyze your images immediately to improve your shooting technique, you

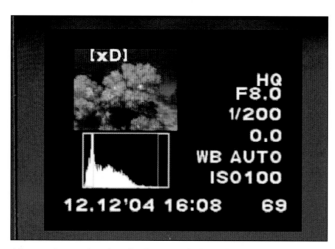

More advanced point & shoot and digital SLR cameras will include a histogram during shooting and preview. This histogram graph indicates when your exposure is too low or exceeds what the image sensor can capture.

can enable this EXIF metadata on playback. With this function, the image in the viewer will be smaller so that you can see the histogram and EXIF metadata in the preview window at the same time. Since not all the data can be shown on the LCD monitor, the most critical is previewed. Typically, values for shutter speed, f/stop, ISO settings, white balance, and compression settings will be shown.

CUSTOM PRESETS

With this menu, you can save out certain menu settings as your favorites. Recalling one of these custom settings will change all the camera functions to that setting. This is a great setting if you want to shoot super-macro and wide-angle on the same dive and don't want to worry about switching all the settings from one subject to the next. For example, you might have a custom 1 setting with a flash white balance, f/8 at $\frac{1}{250}$ second at ISO 100 for super macro, and a custom 2 wide-angle setting of cloudy white balance, f/4 at $\frac{1}{125}$ second at ISO 400. Simply toggling between custom 1 and 2 would change all these values in just a couple of seconds. Best of all, you can preset these values before the dive and not worry about them once you are underwater.

NOISE REDUCTION

Long exposures with digital cameras generally cause a small amount of digital noise. The solution is to go to a submenu and activate the digital noise-reduction fea-

ture. When enabled, it will look for small hot spots in the background and blend them into the image.

PANORAMA

The panorama function sets up a preview screen that allows you to visually align one portion of the panorama to the next. Cameras that offer this function will include software that allows you to stitch the images together into one panoramic image.

BLACK & WHITE OR SEPIA

This menu will allow you to set the camera so that it will shoot in black & white or sepia. This feature is designed for those underwater situations where the color is very monochromatic blue or green, and therefore has no real image value.

We agree that many available light images look better in black & white, but we disagree on using this method to accomplish the task. We have found that it is

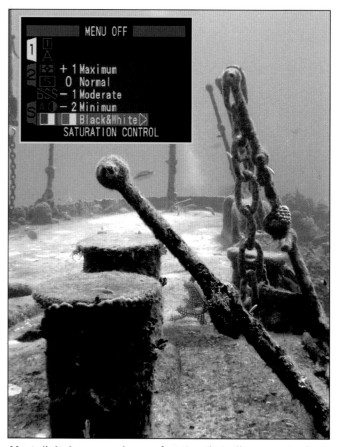

Most digital cameras have a function that allows you to shoot black & white images underwater. If you are diving on a wreck or in deep water where there is virtually no color, you might consider using this function.

still better to shoot the images in color, then convert them to black & white with the converter in your favorite editing program. Most of these programs offer better conversions than the camera's black & white function—and you may later find that you actually like the color version better anyway.

There are also special black & white plug-in filters for Adobe Photoshop that can simulate a wide variety of black & white film and printing paper. Therefore, you have plenty of options beyond camera conversion.

■ COMPOSITION GRID

This grid is one of the options found in the monitor menus, and it will place a grid over your image dividing it into thirds vertically and horizontally. This is designed to help you find the optimum composition. When you find a single subject on a patterned background such as coral, blue water, or a bed of sea anemones, it makes it easy to place the primary subject at one of the points at which these grid lines intersect.

■ VIDEO

When digital cameras first came out, the movie function was limited to 352x240 pixels—which is one quarter of video resolution. These videos looked good on the Internet, but previewed poorly on television sets. Today, many digital cameras offer a second resolution setting for video that is equal in quality (640x480 pixels, 30 frames per second) to many underwater video cameras. This is a great function for those active scenes that just don't look good in the still format. If you are planning on creating a digital presentation using your digital still images, a few video clips shot using the same camera will spice it up.

■ FILE NAMING

The file-naming function usually allows you to reset the file numbers or have consecutive numbering. If you leave it in the reset mode, the file names will be the same from dive to dive, which makes it very difficult to keep from overwriting one file with another with the

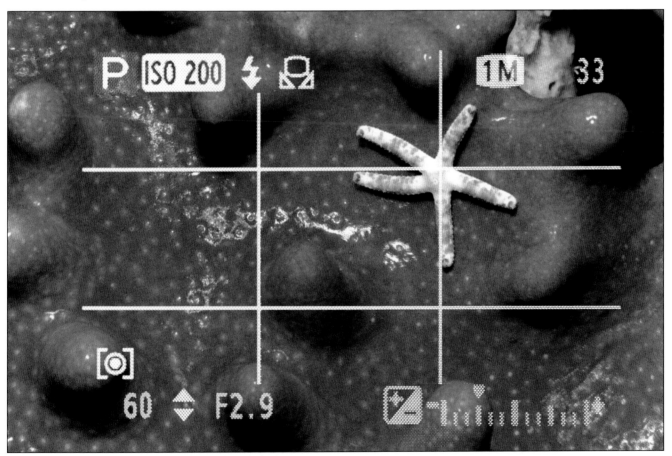

Some digital cameras now sport a composition grid showing four points of intersection. By placing your subject at one of these intersection points, you will find your image has better composition.

same name and number. Most consecutive numbering systems will number up to 10,000 and then roll over to 1 again. This reduces the chances of overwriting a file name since the number 1 will not reappear on your camera for months or years, depending on how often you use your camera.

■ DIGITAL VS. OPTICAL ZOOM

This is one time when the word "digital" is *bad*. Optical zoom uses the range of the optical elements inside the camera to create wide-angle and telephoto effects. The digital zoom, on the other hand, does nothing more than crop the image so that it appears as if you are zooming in on the subject. In effect, the more you use the digital zoom, the lower the quality becomes—until it almost becomes Internet quality. If you want to zoom in on an image by cropping, do it in your editing program. Thankfully, the digital-zoom default setting on most camera systems is off—but if not, be sure this function stays off permanently.

■ LCD MONITOR CONTROL

Most digital cameras have a monitor button on the back of the camera. By pressing it, you can cycle from full display with all the menu text, to a screen that has an image but no menu text, to a blank screen (which saves battery power). If you find that your monitor brightness does not reflect the image brightness found on your calibrated computer monitor, this is also where you would adjust it to match.

■ REAL-TIME MANUAL EXPOSURE

One of the most unusual controls we have seen is a manual exposure control that allows you to adjust the f/stop and shutter speed while previewing the image on the LCD viewer. If the viewer is dark, you can either open the aperture or reduce the shutter speed. As you make the adjustment, the image becomes brighter and brighter. You can continue adjusting until the image looks good. Once it does, you can then take the picture and be assured that you have a correct exposure. In reality, it makes a manual exposure semi-automatic, since your eye has become the exposure meter.

■ SETUP MENUS

These menus vary from camera to camera but generally allow you to set the time and date, format memory cards, reset all camera functions, select user language, add sound effects, and even feature a splash screen for turning the camera on and off. Did we mention that there is also menu for adding the kitchen sink?

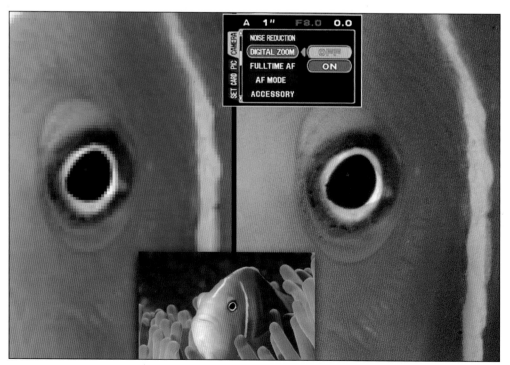

The digital zoom function should never be used. Luckily the default setting is off—and it should stay that way. The image on the left was made using digital zoom, while the image on the right was shot using the optical lens setting.

6. Making the First Dive with Your Digital Camera

We bet that you are going to think this sounds crazy, but the secret to getting good underwater images is *not to go underwater*. The biggest mistake new underwater digital photographers make is to buy a new camera, schedule a dive trip, and take the new camera on a dive. This only leads to frustration, mediocre images, and lots of swearing heard though the regulator.

■ PRACTICE TOPSIDE FIRST

The best way to learn how your new camera works is to shoot with it topside, becoming familiar with all its functions. Then, eventually, take it underwater.

This means that you should take your camera out and photograph flowers to help hone your close-up skills. Trying to digitally capture your active pets will help you become a better fish photographer. Practice working with shutter lag by panning, and photographing a dog or child running in the yard. You will become more adept at taking wide-angle photos underwater by composing topside landscape images. Work with different types of lighting to see their varying effect. Experiment with sunlight, shade, flash, and low light before you ever even think about donning mask, fins, and snorkel. Use an external flash at different angles when shooting close-ups. Include front lighting, side lighting, top lighting, and back lighting. Find out what ISO speeds work the best for the different setups.

Learn the camera controls you'll use regularly and become very familiar with them all. You need to be able to close your eyes and find each specific control.

■ ADDING THE HOUSING

Now put the camera in the housing and repeat the process. It may look strange to your neighbors that you are taking pictures in your garden using your underwater housing, but what the heck? By this time, you should know where most of the controls are located, so they should be easy to find on the housing. Make sure the camera and housing fit comfortably in your hand and that the camera syncs with the external flash system. Although all these measures may seem a bit silly, you will be grateful once you are underwater and find your digital photography is easier because of it.

■ HOUSING MAINTENANCE

Before your first dive using your new camera and housing, you should go through the entire housing checking to make sure each O-ring is clean and greased properly. Most camera housings today include their own

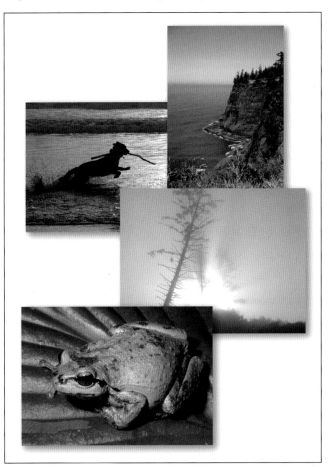

Before taking your digital camera underwater, become familiar with its operation while taking topside images. Practice with lighting, capturing the action, and close-up images.

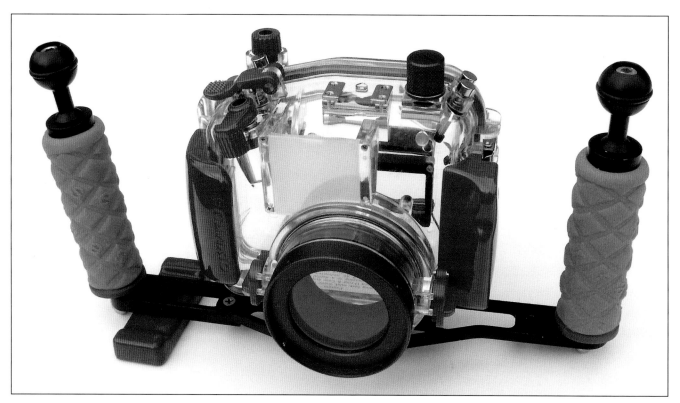

ABOVE—When you buy a new digital camera housing, we recommend that you take the empty housing to at least 60 feet and press all the buttons and levers. This will ensure that the housing will stay dry and protect your fragile digital camera on the next dive. RIGHT—Assemble your system before you go on your first dive trip. Make sure that you have all the parts and that the camera and housing work well together.

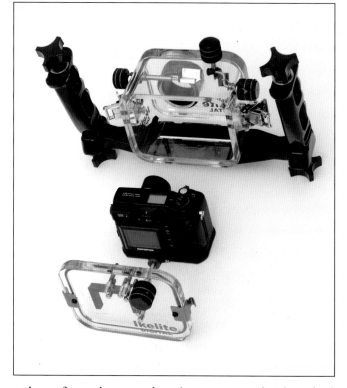

type of O-ring grease that should be used instead of generic brands. How much O-ring grease is needed depends on which professional photographer you ask. Some will tell you that the camera will flood is you use too much grease, others say to use plenty. The truth is that too much grease isn't what floods a camera, but rather the particles that the grease attracts. We like to put on just enough so you can barely feel that it is greased but it slips easily through our fingers. We use a high-powered magnifier to check all surfaces before closing the housing. Once you grease a housing O-ring, be sure to quickly close the housing. Don't leave it open waiting for something to fall on the O-ring.

When you reach your dive location, we recommend that you take the freshly greased, empty housing on a test dive down to over 60 feet if possible. Push and move all the controls, making sure they all operate properly without any leaks. This procedure is generally only performed on new housings, or ones that have had a manufacturer's maintenance overhaul. Although you might view this recommendation as a bit paranoid, it has saved us much heartache. There is nothing worse than having a housing flood on the first day of your two-week dive trip!

We check all the exposed O-rings carefully before each dive trip to make sure none need replacing. Then our rule of thumb is to remove all the surface O-rings every three days for full cleaning. The only exception is if the housing was used in very sandy conditions—and especially if it was set down in the sand. Then, we remove and check all the surface O-rings before making another dive. Sand has a nasty habit of creeping in and invading O-rings. You will find more on camera maintenance in chapter 18.

■ LET'S GO DIVING!

When you have mastered the digital camera on land and your camera's housing has been tested to eliminate potential floods, you are ready for your first digital dive. One of the best places to start is by setting the camera to the program mode and shooting with the flash off.

Take several available-light images of your dive buddy, the reef, and schools of swimming fish. Point the camera up toward the surface, hold it level, and point it downward to see how the metering works at the three angles. Use the exposure compensation if necessary to balance each image at the different angles.

■ USING THE FLASH

Turn on the auxiliary flash and try a few exposures with the flash at a 45-degree angle to your subject. Then try moving the flash above the subject or over the camera to see the effect. If you are not happy with the results, here is quick course in Lighting 101.

One of the best ways to see the effect of the strobe is to use a wide-angle lens and attach the strobe to a long flash arm. Place the flash head so that it is just barely visible in the edge of your pictures. Take several

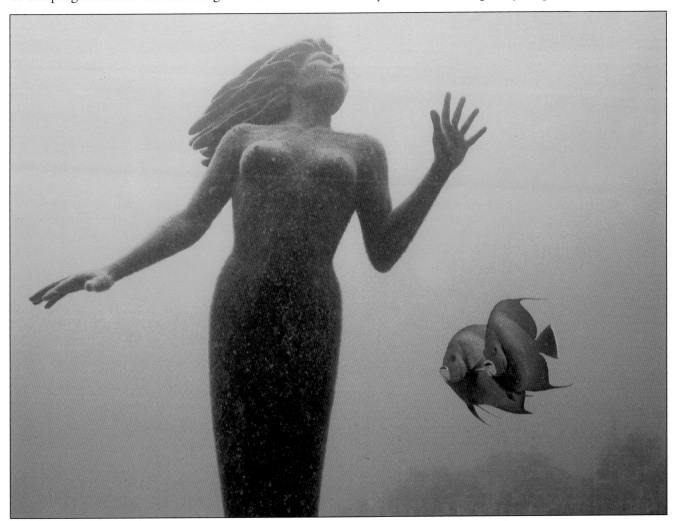

One of your first underwater images should be made with ambient light using the program mode. Adjust the exposure using the exposure compensation menu or button until the exposure is just right.

images, adjusting your exposure each time to see how the flash lights the scene. Move the flash to different angles to see different lighting effects, remembering to keep the head visible in the frame. When you see a lighting pattern you like, move the flash so that it is barely out of the scene and push the shutter.

■ SHOULD YOU DELETE IMAGES?

As you start to take your first underwater images there will be a tendency to delete the bad ones. Don't waste your precious underwater time deleting—just keep shooting. Be sure to use a large enough memory card to enable you keep both the good and problem images.

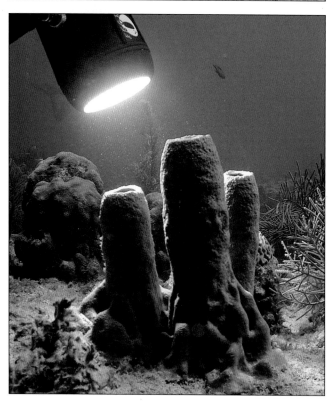

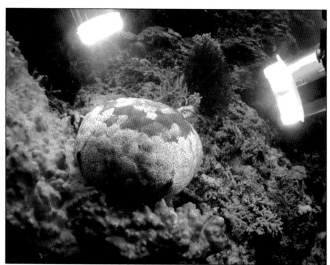

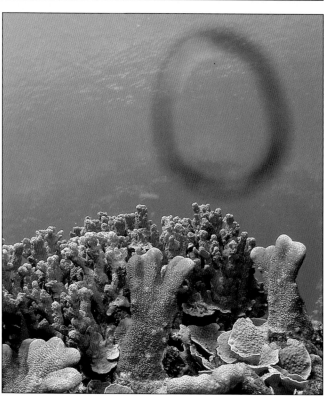

TOP LEFT—The most common placement of the flash is at a 45-degree angle to the camera. We have placed the flash in the image so you can see the relationship of the flash to the subject. BOTTOM LEFT—Don't be afraid to move the flash to different angles to create different types of lighting moods. TOP RIGHT—A twin-flash system provides more even lighting and control over exposure. Again, we have placed both flash units in the image so you can see the position of each. BOTTOM RIGHT—If you see this type of out-of-focus oval shape in your image, it is probably due to a trapped air bubble between your wet lens and housing. You should always remove the wet lens once you are underwater and clear any air bubbles.

SRA—SHOOT, REVIEW, ADJUST

The most important part of digital underwater photography to remember is SRA—Shoot, Review, Adjust. That is what makes digital photography so great. It's like having a photography course underwater—and you are your own teacher. Learn from your mistakes, build on your techniques, and the results will be some great underwater images.

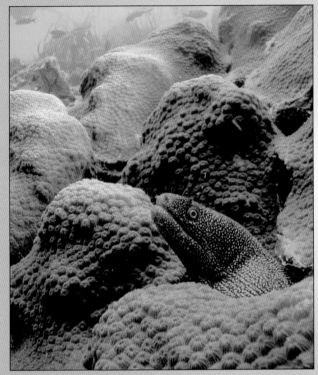

The concept of shoot, review, and adjust (SRA), is shown here with this moray eel. It is obvious here that the flash is incorrectly pointed and is not lighting the subject.

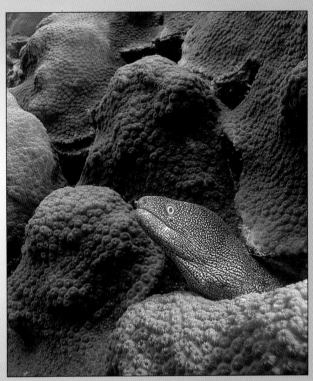

After reviewing the LCD image, the flash was moved to a new position and a new photo was taken with the correct lighting on the subject.

By keeping *all* your images, you can review the EXIF data embedded in the file and see what you did *right* on those images that look good and what went *wrong* on the problem ones. This data will also help you determine the best f/stops, shutter speeds, and ISO settings.

Do not completely trust the image you see on the LCD viewer on the back of the camera. Varying water and lighting conditions may factor in the image output. What looked sharp on the viewer underwater may indeed be out of focus because you were too close. Images that looked overexposed on the viewer may not be as bad as you thought when reviewed on a computer screen. Keep all the files, and delete the ones you don't want later. The only time we delete files under-

water is when we have filled up a memory card and we run into a great subject. Then we quickly have to decide which images are dispensable.

You should also keep in mind that digital cameras take longer to shoot images. That is just a shortcoming of some digital cameras, but new innovations are forthcoming. Don't get impatient when the shutter doesn't fire right away. Instead, practice your digital skills on stationary subjects at first. Many macro subjects do not move very fast, so you will have plenty of time for the camera to lock in on the correct focus and exposure. If the subject is moving, pan the camera with it, squeeze the shutter, and wait for the camera to fire.

7. Getting Good Exposures

The most difficult aspect of underwater photography is achieving correct exposure. It has been a problem from the very beginning of underwater photography, and still is today. Even with all the incredible technological advancements, Mother Nature still has the upper hand, even underwater. There are so many variables that influence exposure underwater, that there is no clear-cut solution.

■ TESTING

Before digital came along, photographers spent many dives testing, creating charts, and working on exposure rulers . . . only to start over conducting even *more* tests when a new variable was introduced. For every lens or flash introduction, and each new film emulsion, the testing process started over again.

When it comes to exposure, the only difference between film and digital is that you can take more bad

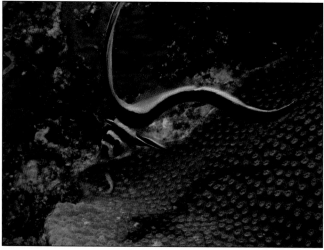

RIGHT—Upon review of this point & shoot digital image, it was determined that that f/8 was too small an aperture. BELOW— The f/stop was opened to f/5.6 and we achieved a much better exposure.

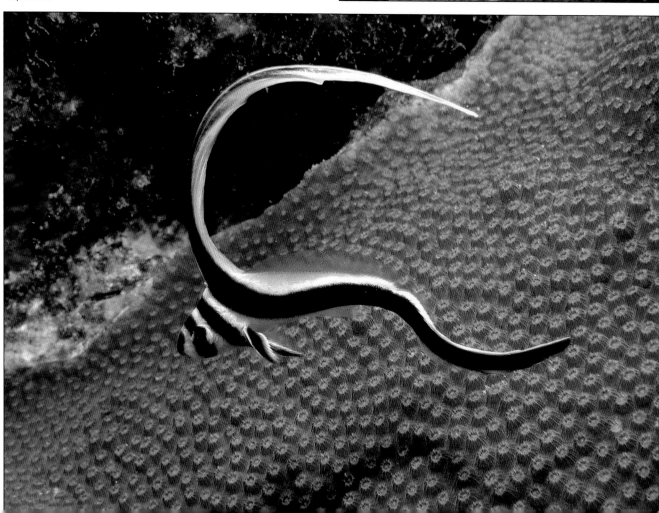

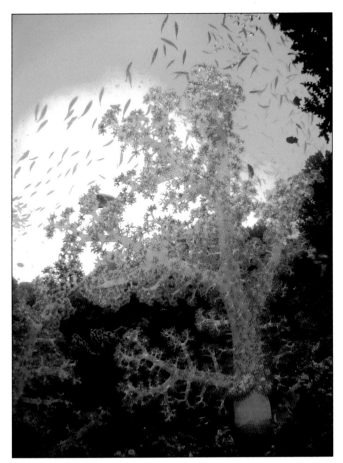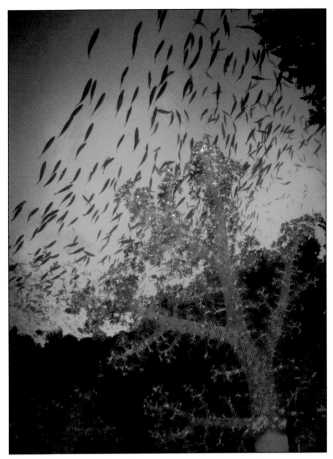

LEFT—This soft coral image taken in the Solomons resulted in blooming due to incorrect shutter speed. RIGHT—Keeping the f/stop and flash output the same, we increased the shutter speed to reduce the background exposure and remove the blooming effect.

exposures with digital than with film. Digital has a very big advantage in that when you get a bad exposure, you see it a second later on the camera's LCD. You can then keep adjusting and correcting the image until you get a good exposure. So, when you hear about a digital photographer who just shot 150 exposures on a dive, remember that at least 75 of them are probably *bad*. The difference is that 75 are probably *good*, which is quite an improvement over 36.

So what really makes a good exposure? In the film world it is when you can take your image and make a good print that holds detail in both the highlights and shadows. If your image is a little underexposed with slide film or a little overexposed with color negative film, you are still fine. With digital, you'll need rather exacting standards to produce good exposures.

■ THE BLOOMING EFFECT

In digital photography, when the exposure exceeds what the chip can physically record, it will bloom out and make a pure white hole in the image where there is no data. This is a big problem underwater when you take a wide-angle picture into the sun. Blooming is also one of the biggest complaints professional photographers have about digital.

There are actually two reasons for this blooming effect. Blooming occurs when the light level striking the sensor chip exceeds what the chip can record. The smaller the physical size of the chip, the greater the blooming. As the concentration of pixels increases on the same size chip the blooming will increase proportionately, so that an SLR has less blooming than a point & shoot camera.

Blooming can also occur when you go below 30 feet and there is no longer any red visible light in the scene. Film can record thousands of levels of red, green, and blue, while most digital camera sensors only record 256 levels of each color. Digital records the variations between red, green, and blue perfectly, while film is not so exacting and blends one color to the next to achieve a good exposure. The result is that with film you can shoot directly into the sun and maintain a smooth color gradation.

So is there anything you can do to avoid blooming when using digital? Many of the more advanced digital cameras, especially the digital SLRs, have a built-in histogram to tell you when you are getting overexposures and losing data. This camera histogram is much like the one in Adobe Photoshop with a line chart that shows how the detail fits into the shadows, midtones, and highlights. When the data extends right up to the edge of the highlight side of the histogram, your image will have blooming and will be unusable. One solution is to reduce the exposure until it correctly fits within the histogram.

With digital cameras, you can also reduce the blooming problem by taking images only from 0 to 30 feet. This way there is still some red in the image and the sensor can compensate. Keep reducing the exposure until you no longer see the blooming effect on the LCD screen. This method, used in conjunction with the histogram, is your best bet.

When the sun is out and you try to take images below 30 feet, you will probably experience the blooming effect with most digital cameras. If you want to shoot below 30 feet, try to take pictures on overcast days, when the lighting ratio is not so extreme. Another solution is to place a diver or other subject between yourself and the sun to block the direct sunlight.

New technologies are coming out that expand the exposure range of electronic sensors, so the blooming effect will eventually be solved. We have seen great improvements in minimizing blooming starting with Fuji's fourth-generation CCD chips. Until the problem is permanently solved, however, you can also try using the RAW file format, reducing the contrast and/or saturation, or bracketing your exposure. With these bracketed exposures, you can also use the new High Dynamic Range function found in Photoshop CS2 to extend the range of your image to help reduce the blooming effect.

■ PHOTOGRAPHIC EXPOSURE 101

This brings us to the most basic level of photography: Photographic Exposure 101. This may be old hat to many of you, but since this is a photography book, we need to cover it.

Aperture. The aperture is the diameter of the lens opening through which the light passes and is captured on the light-sensitive sensor array inside the camera. As the aperture gets smaller (larger number), less light passes through the lens. The f/stop scale on point & shoot cameras generally starts at f/2.8 and continues with values at 4, 5.6, 8, and 11. With digital SLRs, this f/stop scale starts at f/2.8 and can extend to f/11 to 22 or 32.

Shutter Speed. The shutter in the camera controls the length of time that the light strikes the sensor array. Shutter speeds with most point & shoot digital cameras will start at 30 seconds and continue with 15, 8, 4, 2, 1, $\frac{1}{2}$, $\frac{1}{4}$, $\frac{1}{8}$, $\frac{1}{15}$, $\frac{1}{30}$, $\frac{1}{60}$, $\frac{1}{125}$, $\frac{1}{250}$, $\frac{1}{500}$, $\frac{1}{1000}$, and $\frac{1}{2000}$ sec-

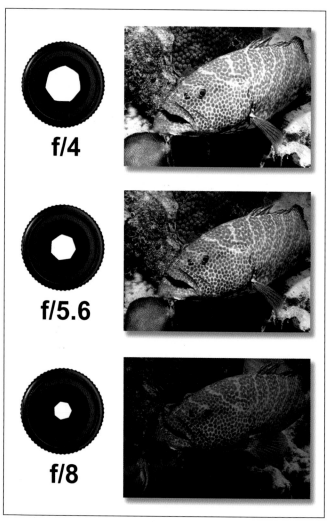

This diagram shows the relationship of the lens apertures to the image exposure. Note that each full f/stop of change will half or double the exposure output.

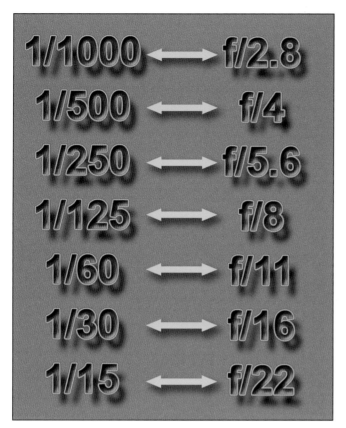

This chart shows the relationship between shutter speed and f/stop. Each combination results in the same exposure. As you reduce a value by one half, the other side doubles.

onds. Digital SLR shutter speeds vary from camera to camera, but we have seen shutter extensions on the high side at $\frac{1}{4000}$ second and $\frac{1}{8000}$ second.

Halving and Doubling. Each step *up* in aperture value halves the light; each step *down* the scale doubles the light. A benefit of smaller apertures is an increase in depth of field. As the shutter speed increases from one value to the next it gets progressively shorter and the light level drops by half with each step. The opposite is true when you decrease the shutter speed (making it longer). A benefit of higher shutter speeds is that it stops the action and creates sharper images. Both the aperture and shutter speed must work hand-in-hand to achieve a good exposure. Therefore, it becomes a juggling act with f/stops and shutter speeds to obtain a good exposure while still maintaining depth of field and image sharpness.

When you have achieved a good available-light exposure, you can modify one variable if you compensate by changing the other one. For example, if you have a good exposure at $\frac{1}{125}$ second at f/8, you can still

maintain a good exposure if you increase the shutter speed to $\frac{1}{250}$ (halving the amount of light) and open the aperture to f/5.6 (doubling the amount of light). Since one adjustment halves the light and the other doubles it, the net change in the amount of light is zero—so your exposure will be exactly the same as at the previous shutter speed and aperture combination.

Flash exposure is a totally different ball game. Flash exposure will be covered in depth in the manual exposure section of this chapter, and also in chapter 9 on flash systems.

◼ ISO RATING
Another exposure control that you have with your digital camera is the ISO setting. In the film world, the silver halide crystals with a higher rating are more sensitive to light. So when you need to stop the action or photograph in low light, you just use a higher ISO film.

With digital cameras, the ISO setting adjusts the electrical charge on the image-sensor chip so that it is more or less sensitive. It uses the familiar ISO terms that we photographers are accustom to using. When the light level gets low, the action increases, or you need more depth of field, changing apertures and shutter speeds may not always be adequate. The solution is to increase the ISO speed until you have acceptable parameters for your camera's aperture and shutter speed. A big advantage with digital is that you can adjust this ISO setting from image to image.

◼ EXPOSURE MODES
When you combine all this basic photographic technology with the new high technology of digital cameras, you end up with an exposure system called PASM. It may sound like a strange word, but you will see it on the top of your digital camera as part of the exposure mode dial. The P stands for program exposure, the A for aperture priority, the S for shutter priority, and the M stands for manual exposure. Most professionals teaching photography would tell you to forget the first three and use only manual. We think it's only fair that you are given a chance to understand all these controls and then make your own decision.

Program Mode. The program mode is an automated exposure mode that allows the camera to pick the

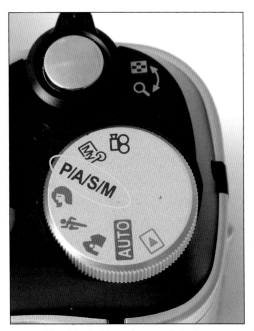

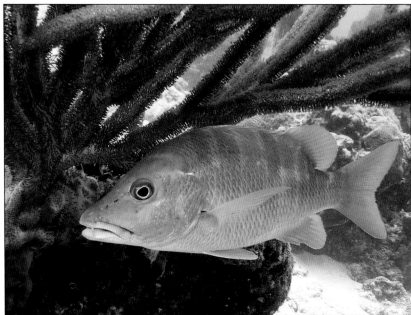

LEFT—The P/A/S/M setting on digital cameras allows you to select program, aperture, shutter, or manual exposure modes. RIGHT— In the program mode, the camera does it all. It calculates both shutter speed and aperture, and even balances flash fill.

f/stop and shutter speed combinations that will result in a good exposure. If you want to adjust either of the two values, you can rotate an exposure control dial on the back of the camera and it will halve one and double the other. This allows you to make the necessary adjustment and still maintain a good exposure. For example, let's say you are in program mode in shallow water with a wide-angle lens, and the exposure is $\frac{1}{30}$ second at f/8. Since wide-angle lenses have plenty of depth of field, the f/8 is more than you need but the shutter speed is low. You may have a good exposure, but it may be a blurry one. All you have to do is rotate the exposure dial one click and the camera will change the exposure to $\frac{1}{60}$ second at f/5.6. Rotating the exposure dial two clicks will give you $\frac{1}{125}$ second at f/4.

Program mode is best suited for available-light photography, since you have full control of shutter speed and f/stop. If the overall image is dark or light because of white sand or deep blue water, you can bias the program mode using the exposure-compensation dial we discussed earlier in chapter 5. We find the program mode especially useful when we are returning to the beach, dock, or back to the boat, and the bright sun at the shallow depth hinders our view of the LCD screen. In the Program mode, if you frame it right, your exposure should be okay.

Aperture-Priority Mode. Switching to the aperture-priority mode with available light allows you to select the f/stop you want to use to achieve a specific depth of field, while the camera picks the necessary shutter speed. You can also bias the aperture-priority control with the exposure-compensation dial.

In this mode, if you turn on a flash with a digital SLR, all bets are off. The camera's shutter speed will stop at the highest flash sync, and it will not budge any lower. Using an SLR to create wide-angle image with flash in the aperture-priority mode is difficult and will often result in an exposure imbalance between the background and foreground. On the other hand, using aperture priority with macro lenses and an SLR works fine, because you are working with small apertures and generally you don't care if the background is dark. Since the aperture also controls the flash exposure and depth of field, it is actually ideal for macro work.

Digital point & shoot cameras are somewhat different. If you use aperture priority with the flash off, the camera will set a corresponding shutter speed that will provide a correct available-light exposure. If you change the f/stop, the camera will then adjust the shutter speed to compensate and still give a correct exposure. When you turn the flash on, the more basic level of digital point & shoot camera will just fire the flash at full power, and this may over- or underexpose your image. Some of the more advanced point & shoot cameras use sensor systems to measure distance and ISO speed in order to achieve a correct flash exposure at that distance. The only way to tell exactly what your camera will do in the aperture-priority mode is to check your instruction manual or run flash tests on land, taking images of the same subject at varying distances. If the camera adjusts the flash to provide a correct exposure, then you are set. If not, then you will have to change the ISO speed, flash compensation setting, or power control on the back of the flash to achieve correct flash exposure. Once you do, the aperture priority mode should then give you both good available light and flash exposures. Keep in mind that point & shoots do not have the flash-sync restrictions that you find in digital and film SLR cameras. This means that whether you turn the flash on or off, the digital point & shoot camera will go through the full range of shutter speeds to compensate for changes in aperture settings.

Shutter-Priority Mode. Shutter priority is an exposure mode that lets you select the shutter speed needed to control the action, while the camera sets the aperture to provide a correct exposure. This mode is an excellent tool when you must have a high shutter speed to stop the motion of a large swimming animal. You have the

Macro and close-up photographers will use the aperture-priority mode to select apertures that provide satisfactory depth of field.

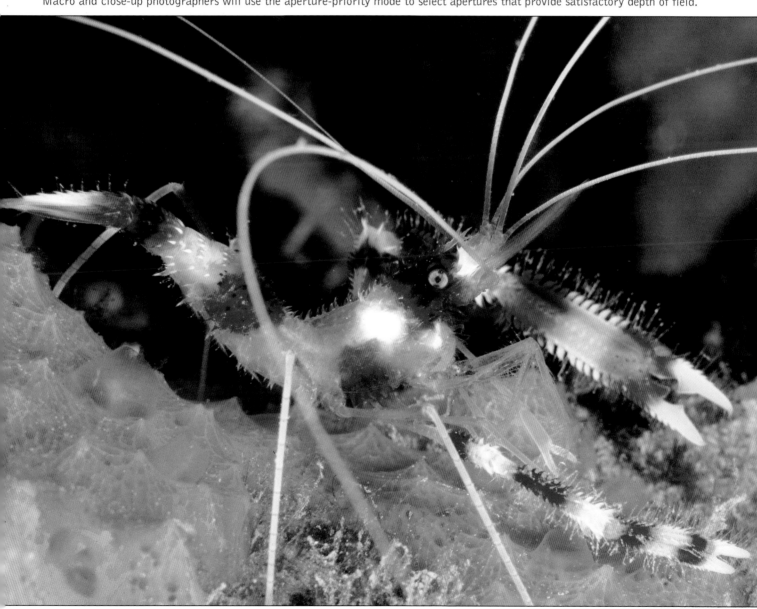

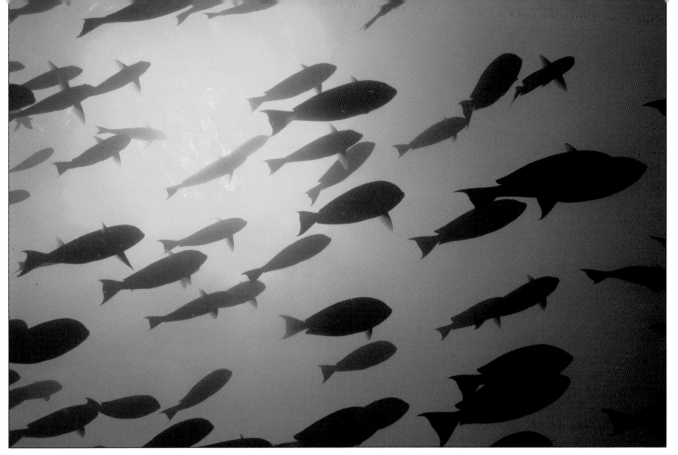

When the action increases, you can use the shutter-priority mode to select a shutter speed that will stop that action. The camera will then pick the corresponding f/stop to provide a correct exposure.

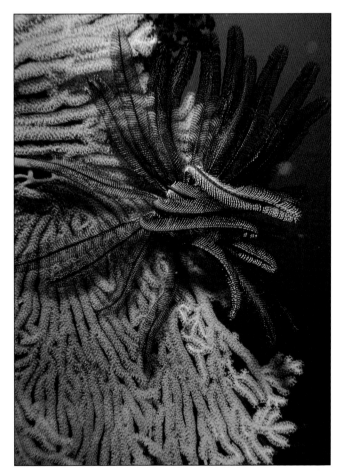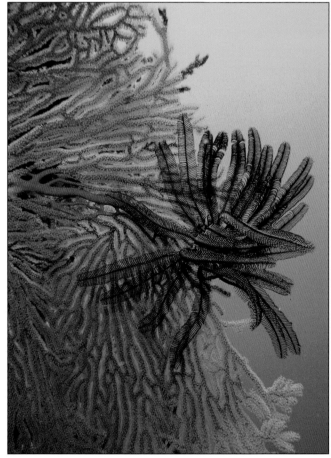

LEFT—When lighting ratios become difficult, you can switch to the manual exposure mode. Here, the f/stop and flash output were adjusted to provide proper exposure to this crinoid. RIGHT—The shutter speed was reduced to lighten the background exposure.

same shutter-speed action control with the program mode if you take the time to rotate the mode dial as the action increases.

Manual Exposure Mode. The underwater photography world has come full circle. In the beginning, the only way to get good exposures with flash was to use manual exposure control. As technology improved, automation came to the underwater camera world and more images were taken automatically. Now, we have entered the digital world. As advanced as digital cameras have become, they still have a very narrow exposure latitude, especially when using an electronic flash underwater. Using the exposure compensation dial and one of the auto modes just doesn't seem to give the real control you need. The auto-exposure systems work well with available light, but most underwater images are taken using flash. What you need is what we started with many years ago: manual exposure. The process is simple. You adjust the f/stop and shutter speed independently of each other to maximize depth of field and still stop the action.

The difference is that, with point & shoot digital cameras, you use a new method of calculating exposure to get a good balance between the background and foreground flash. The first step is to take a picture of the scene you want to balance, then look at the LCD viewer to judge the foreground exposure. If it is light or dark you can adjust it using the camera's f/stop or the power setting on the back of the flash if it has one. If the exposure is still out of range, adjust the ISO speed. One of these three controls should enable you to get a good foreground flash exposure. Then, look at the background exposure. If it is dark, reduce the shutter speed; if it is light, increase the shutter speed. Changing the value of the shutter speed will have very little effect on the foreground exposure until you reach $\frac{1}{1000}$ second. At that point, you may have to bump up the foreground exposure a small amount to compensate for the reciprocity failure of the chip at high shutter speeds.

If you are using a digital SLR camera and wide-angle lenses, you are restricted to the same rules of exposure balance used by film SLR photographers. Since the shutter speed is restricted to the flash-sync speed when you use flash, you have to balance the background exposure with the f/stop. Then, adjust the flash power or distance to achieve a good foreground exposure. Digital SLRs still have a big advantage over film cameras, because you can preview your image to see if you got it right. Film photographers have to rely on experience and testing to obtain the same results.

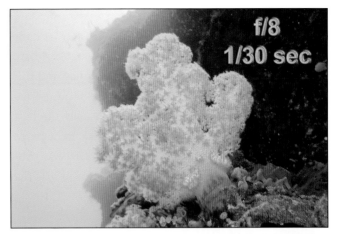

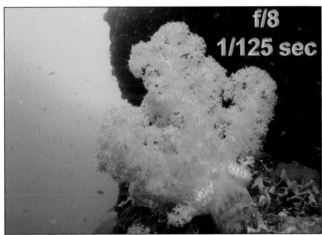

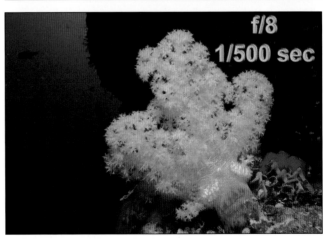

Balancing the flash foreground exposure with the ambient light, can create some varied effects. We first adjusted the foreground exposure using the variable power setting on the back of the flash. By changing the shutter speed to higher and lower settings, the background varied in its intensity.

8. Available-Light Photography

Some of the most striking underwater photos showing the vastness of the underwater world are made using only available light. You may find this one of the best places to start your digital-photography journey. Available-light photography is usually the best choice when the water is very dirty, since it helps to avoid backscatter. It also best when the underwater subjects are very large or your dive is deep enough that the light level and colors are reduced.

■ EXPOSURE METHODS

Since most available-light images are, in essence, underwater landscapes, you will want to start by use a wide-angle lens. The digital SLR camera and housing will need a super-wide lens and dome port to minimize the distortion.

Exposure is easy since you only have to worry about one light source: the sun. The best method for exposure in available light is with the program mode. You can rotate the selection dial to get different combinations of f/stops and shutter speeds. If the exposure is too light or dark, you merely go to the exposure compensation dial and add or subtract exposure from the scene.

This school of sea lions at Santa Barbara Island was photographed on color negative film with a Nikonos 5 camera and 15mm lens. Because this photo was taken at a shallow depth, it produced a colorful image without the use of flash.

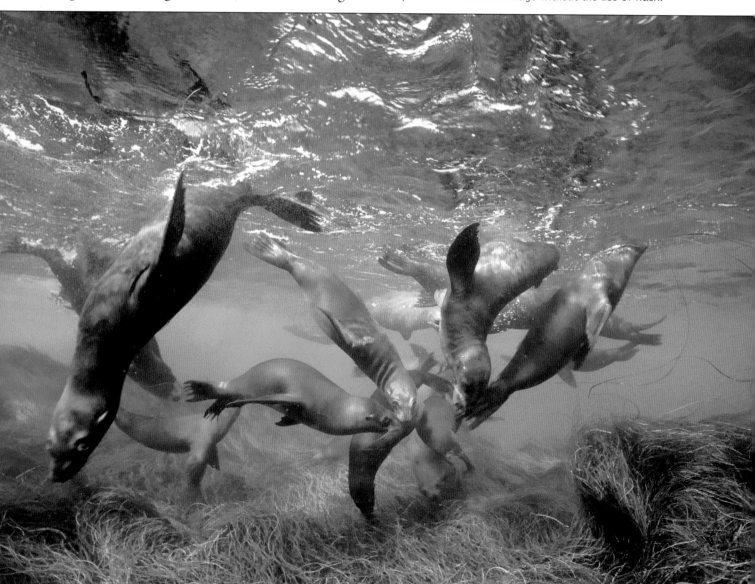

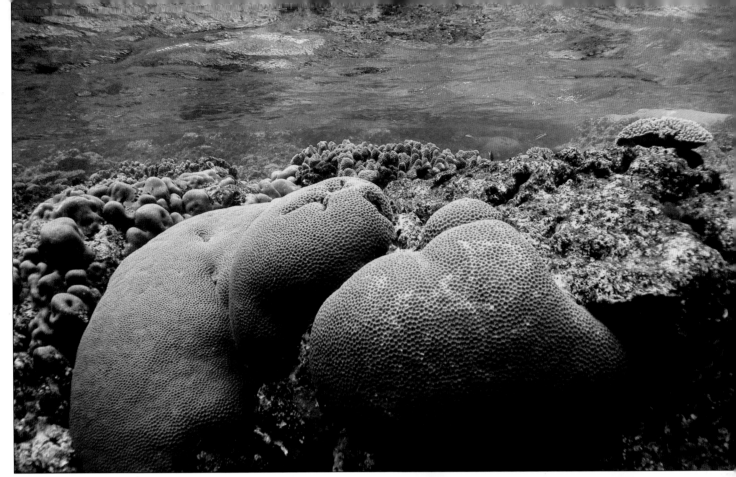

LEFT—The digital camera was set to custom white balance to produce this colorful panoramic image without the use of any external light source. RIGHT—You can bias the color balance of your digital camera even more by using special warming filters that provide control over color loss at depth.

If you find that you are constantly adjusting the compensation dial, you might consider another option. Press the shutter down halfway as you point the camera at a light level you want to record, and then swing it back for the final exposure. When you press the shutter down all the way, it will use the exposure you metered when the shutter was pressed halfway down.

If the preview is still wrong, you can change the metering view with the shutter down halfway to a brighter or darker area to capture a better exposure. If you find it too hard to press the shutter down just half way without shooting a picture, you should consider using the exposure lock. It works in the same way except that it is separate button from the shutter.

■ POINT OF VIEW

You can create a completely different feel with your available-light images by taking several images from the

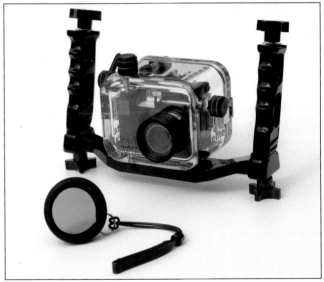

same position, but take each from a different point of view. Pointing the camera at an upward angle is the most popular available-light point of view. It will almost always create a silhouette view of whatever is situated between you and the sun. Divers and large animals like sharks and whales make great silhouette images. Be sure to vary the subject's position in the frame to enhance the composition. You can read more tips about composition in chapter 15. If you find the silhouette exposure

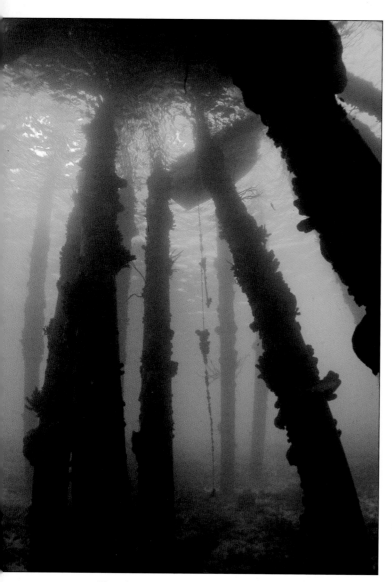

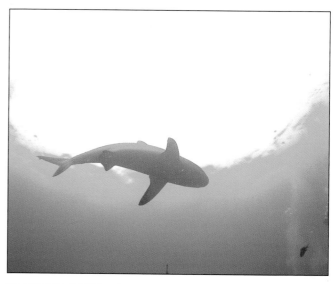

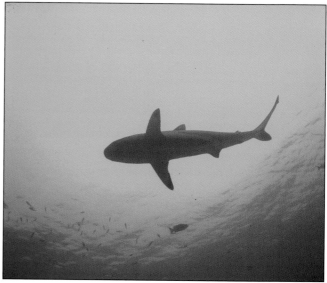

LEFT—Shooting upward in available light can create some very dynamic silhouettes. In this case, the small boat was silhouetted next to the Salt Pier in Bonaire, which added some extra impact. TOP RIGHT—This shark image was taken looking straight up into the sun while using a point & shoot digital camera in the program exposure mode. This blooming effect was cased by too much light striking the camera sensor. BOTTOM RIGHT—By increasing the shutter speed a couple of steps, the blooming effect was removed.

too dark in the LCD viewer, move the camera down slightly, press the shutter down half way or use the exposure lock, then swing the camera back to take your silhouette.

Care must be taken not to overexpose shots taken looking into the sun. Digital cameras have a problem shooting into the sun for silhouettes, because the tonal range is often beyond what the chip can handle. The result will be posterized colors around a white hole. One solution is to keep cutting the exposure down until the blooming effect disappears. For more ideas about reducing blooming refer back to chapter 7.

■ OTHER AVAILABLE-LIGHT OPTIONS

Shooting available-light images midway between up and down will generally give you a smooth-toned background that is very easy to meter for exposure. If you are shooting in very shallow water, turning the camera into a vertical position will give you some very striking images of the ocean floor reflecting off the surface.

Pointing the camera downward makes it difficult to get a usable exposure. Usually, dark subjects against a sandy white background give you the best shot for the downward view. Light objects on a dark ocean floor lack contrast and look much like shots taken at night.

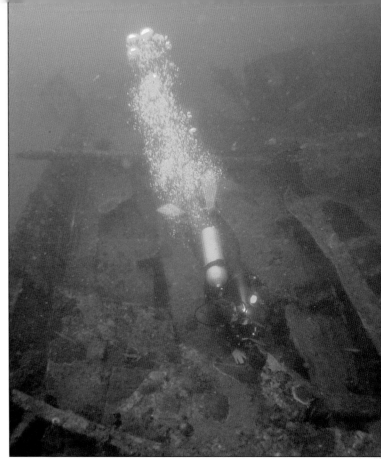

RIGHT—When you shoot down on a subject in ambient light, there is a good chance that your subject will blend in with the ocean floor. BELOW LEFT AND RIGHT—Shooting level in open water can yield some pleasing background tones. These two sea lions were playing catch with this starfish.

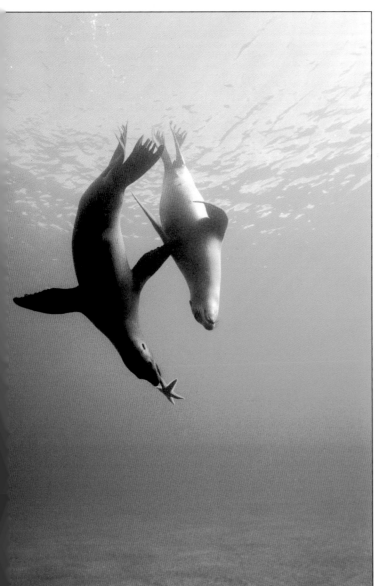

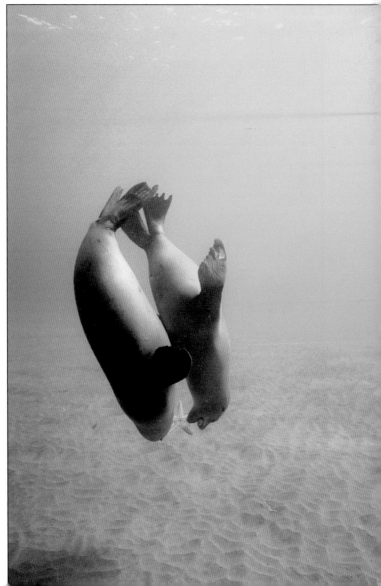

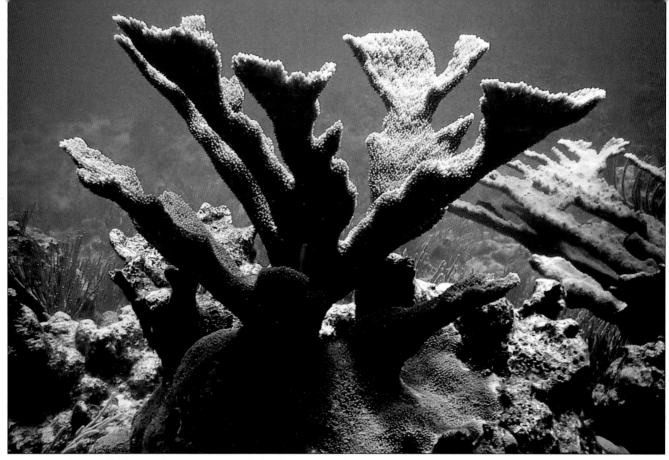

Many digital point & shoot cameras have excellent color control when using the white-balance setting in shallow water.

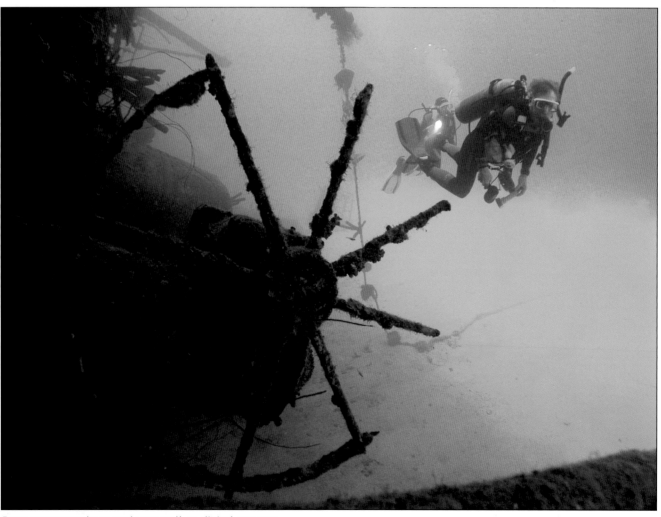

Deep-water wrecks record very well on digital cameras.

SHALLOW WATER

When taking available-light images in shallow water (less than 30 feet), you can create some very colorful images using the white-balance function. You will need to take a white slate or plastic white-balance card that is at least 3" x 3" down on the dive with you. Once you find the scene you want capture, quickly remove your plastic white-balance card from your BC pocket, take a reading, and then use that white balance to record the scene. The colors that you see with your eyes will magically appear on the camera's LCD monitor. You can bias the color even warmer by dropping down a few feet, taking a custom white-balance reading, then coming back up to the shallower depth to take your shot. Since many of the new cameras allow for the storage of several white-balance settings, you could store recordings at several depths, and recall them on later dives.

DEEP WATER

When photographing large objects like shipwrecks in deep water, you should assume that most all of the color in the image will be lost due to the depth. You will have

BLACK & WHITE

Digital cameras can shoot in black & white. However, even when the scene is monochrome, we recommended that you shoot your image in color and convert it later to black & white in your editing program. The exception would be if you know you eventually want to create black & white images but are having trouble visualizing how the scene will look when converted. In this case, try taking one shot in color, then one in black & white using the camera function. Compare the two choices while underwater to see if you like how it looks (the composition, etc.). If you are pleased, continue shooting the rest of your images in full color. That way, you know your shots will work in black & white, but you'll also have the option of using them in color.

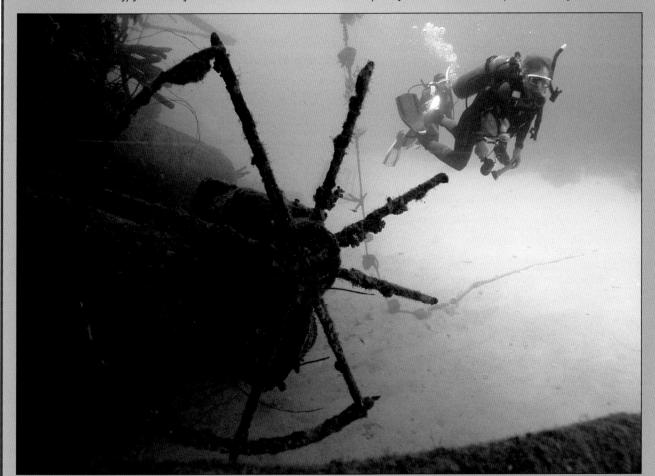

If you don't like the monochrome tone of the deep dive, you can try the black & white setting in the camera or convert your image to black & white later using your image editor. Compare the image above with the one on the facing page (bottom).

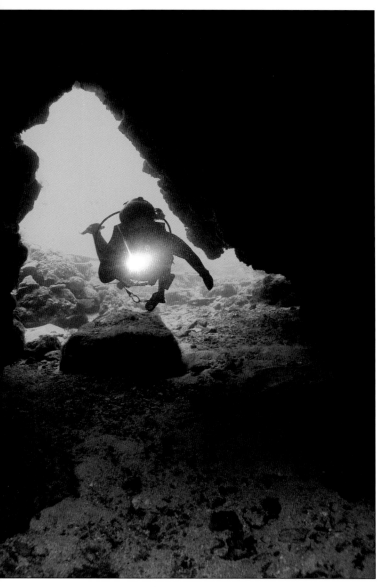

You can add a touch of color by changing the white balance to auto when using a flashlight on a deeper dive. The camera will try to correct the color, giving your flashlight a red hue. If auto doesn't work, try other settings until the red appears.

speeds, but revert to a lower resolution to accomplish the feat.

Rotate the mode dial in the program mode so that the f/stop is at the widest opening. This will increase the shutter speed to its maximum for this light level. Keep in mind that with most wide-angle lenses, you can handhold the camera at $\frac{1}{15}$ second shutter speed and still get a sharp image if you are careful. Brace yourself, if possible, and make sure you gently squeeze the shutter down until it fires. Do not depress it quickly, as this will usually produce a blurred image.

■ FLASHLIGHTS AS PROPS

If you have a dive buddy that is planning on posing for you while you take some available-light shots, have them take a flashlight with them on the dive. When they swim through the photo, have them point the light toward you. You will find that the small accent of light adds a lot of impact to the image. This is a great technique for divers swimming under overhangs and through cave entrances.

The same concept applies when photographing a video photographer at work. When you capture them from the side as they document the ocean floor, you will find that their lights accent the color of the reef. If they use bright tungsten lights, you might consider trying the tungsten white-balance setting. The colors under tungsten light will be balanced, and the background will become even bluer than if you used the sunlight, flash, or custom white-balance settings.

virtually monochromatic colors that may be best converted later to black & white for added impact. You should also be using the highest ISO speed that supports maximum resolution. We say this because there are some digital cameras that support very high ISO

D r. Harold Edgerton's invention of the electronic flash is what brought color to the underwater world of photography. These electronic marvels take a low-voltage battery source, boost it up to a very high voltage, and then discharge it through xenon gas when the camera shutter is depressed. The result is a very bright light source of a very short duration that has the same color balance as the sun. Electronic flash units come in all sizes, beam angles, power output, and with varying power sources.

In previous underwater photography books, readers were presented with pages and pages of charts with flash-guide numbers, beam angles, and methods for calculating exposures. It was not uncommon to see underwater flash units plastered with custom labels showing the different combinations of distance, ISO speeds, and f/stops. These charts usually worked well, as they were derived from extensive flash testing in a wide variety of underwater situations.

Today, however, digital photographers use a completely new approach to underwater flash photography. You no longer need all the charts and guide numbers to calculate your exposure. Electronic flash exposures today are done with the SRA (shoot, review, and adjust) technique that we discussed in previous chapters. This makes it easy to use a flash underwater. Simply turn on the flash, take a picture, view it in the LCD viewer, and adjust the camera or flash until you achieve a correct exposure. This adjustment can be done by altering the f/stop, ISO speed, or power setting on the back of the flash. Because flash-exposure calculation is easier with this visual verification, you can now spend more time

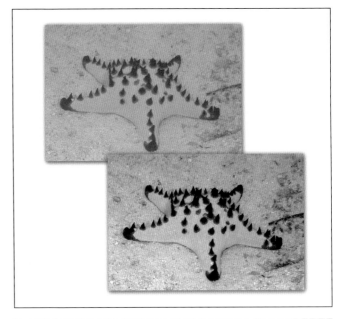

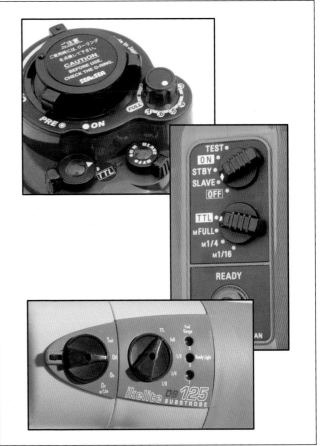

TOP—The electronic flash brings color, saturation, and contrast to a scene (upper left without flash, lower right with flash). BOTTOM—The various levels of flash power can be adjusted using the control panel on the back or side of the flash. The top is Sea & Sea, middle is Nikonos, and the bottom is an Ikelite strobe-control panel.

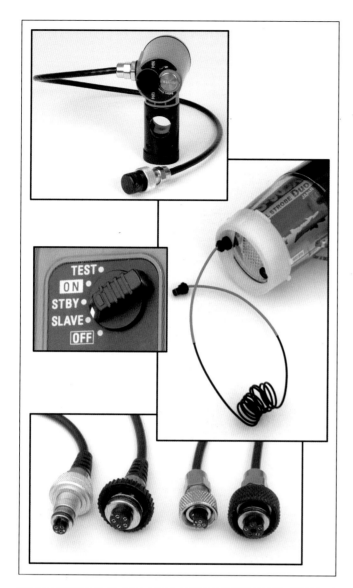

taking advantage of some of the flash's advanced features. This allows you to perfect a wide variety of flash techniques to help improve your shooting style.

To fully understand the potential of the electronic flash, we will take you through its various technical features and show how they can be used to create some great images.

■ TTL, DIGITAL, AUTO, MANUAL

TTL (Through the Lens). The output of an underwater flash unit is controlled in four possible ways. The first is TTL or through-the-lens metering. This means that a both camera and flash talk the same electronic language. This enables the camera's metering system to turn the flash on and off when adequate light strikes the light-sensitive chip inside the camera. You can bias this control using a flash-compensation control often found on the more advanced point & shoot cameras and most digital SLR cameras. This TTL function doesn't work for every type of scene, but it's perfect when the subject

LEFT—Digital cameras have several methods of flash sync. Here are a TTL slave sync from Ikelite (top), slave function on a Nikonos flash (middle left), and an optical cable on a Sea & Sea flash (middle right). The bottom image shows Sea & Sea sync cables (left) and Ikelite sync cables (right). BELOW—Both the new eTTL control board in the digital SLR Ikelite housings (left) and the ROC control panel from Light & Motion (right) are used to override and bias the flash exposure output.

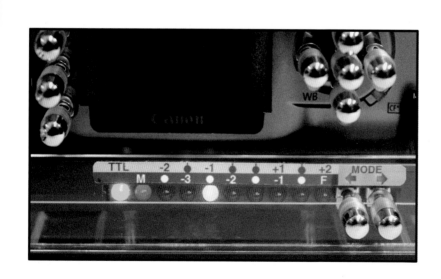

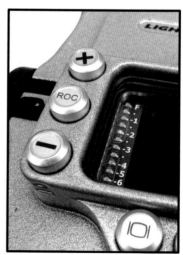

fills most of the frame, as with macro images. It generally will not work very well for wide-angle images if there is too much depth in the scene, as the TTL system cannot get an accurate reading. The TTL flash system often works better with film cameras than digital, because film cameras read the exposure directly off the film. One big advantage of TTL is that any power that is not used is saved for the next shot. This enables flash-recycle times in TTL mode to be almost instantaneous, even with a very large flash.

Digital. Digital flash units are relatively new to the underwater world so there are only a few in existence. This type of flash uses the focus, f/stop, and aperture information supplied by the digital camera and lens to obtain an accurate exposure. Since this system uses the focus point to determine the necessary flash output, it is imperative that focus is locked on the primary subject in the scene. Keep in mind that you must also accurately position your flash to light the main subject, otherwise close objects will be overexposed.

Auto. Automatic flash units use a sensor inside the flash head to calculate the exposure. The f/stop and ISO information is fed from the back of the flash into the sensor so it can determine a good exposure. This type of flash is employed if you want to use a brand-X flash with a brand-Y camera and the language is not compatible.

Manual. Manual flash systems use a dial on the back of the flash to regulate full power or a portion of that power. Early versions of manual flash units often featured full-, half-, and quarter-power settings. Today, we see flash units offering as many as eight power-level settings. That makes this type of flash popular because it provides the photographer optimum control over the final flash output.

Film photographers must use the guide number chart off the back of the manual flash to calculate the exposure. The digital photographer merely shoots, reviews, and adjusts the power to obtain the proper exposure.

■ FLASH SYNC

In order for the camera and flash to fire simultaneously, they must be linked together, but flash sync can be accomplished in several ways. The flash-sync cord is the

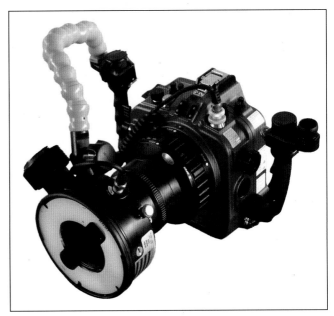

A digital SLR port-mounted flash unit from INON allows even lighting for macro and super-macro photography.

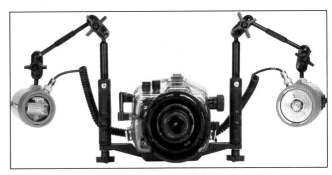

This Ikelite digital SLR housing has twin flash units that are synced to the camera via a double sync cord and dual flash connectors. (Photograph courtesy of Ikelite.)

oldest method and is still the most reliable. With this method, a cable is hooked to the camera and exits the camera housing via an O-ring port. It then connects to the flash via an O-ring port on the back, side, or bottom of the flash. Manual flash units use two wires and contacts to make the proper connection. The TTL and digital flash systems can use up to five wires and contacts to achieve flash sync. The downside to this flash-sync system is that these cables are very susceptible to moisture and will fail if even a minuscule amount of water enters the plug connectors. These cords are bulky and can sometimes get in the way when shooting underwater pictures if they are not secured properly.

The fiber-optic system is relatively new to underwater photography and uses a very small optic cable to trigger the flash. With this system, a small flash inside the housing is fired and the light passes through the cable, triggering the fiber-optic sensor on the external flash. This works extremely well with acrylic point & shoot housings that have an internal flash and no sync port. Simply cover the flash port on the front of the acrylic housing with a special black Velcro patch from Sea & Sea. Then, attach one end of the fiber-optic cable to this patch and the other end to the external flash.

HIGH-SPEED FLASH

When a flash is in TTL, auto, or a partial-manual power mode, the output is controlled by the flash duration. You will find that the lower the power mode, the shorter the flash duration. At full power, most flash units are at $1/1000$ to $1/1500$ second. If you use one of the reduced-power methods mentioned above, the flash duration could be as high as $1/12,000$ second when at $1/16$ power. This increase in speed will result in a sharper image, especially when shooting at extreme macro magnifications. This is one reason that professionals use very large flash units for macro photography. Having massive amounts of power available close in to the subject allows the flash to have a very short duration and very fast recycle time. Another way to boost your flash speed is to increase the ISO so that less flash is needed to illuminate the subject.

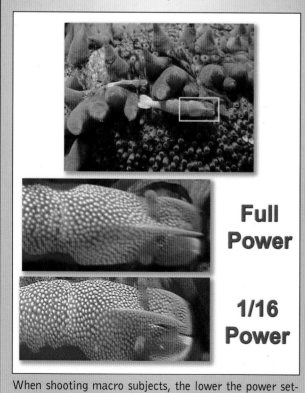

Full Power

1/16 Power

When shooting macro subjects, the lower the power setting, the sharper the image.

This diverts the light to fire the external flash via the optic cable. This fiber-optic cable is waterproof and can be attached or detached while underwater.

Many point & shoot cameras have a pre-flash that is used for focus and exposure control. The flash will then use a pre-flash control to avoid the pre-flash and only use the main flash as a trigger.

The auto TTL digital-flash sensor is a small device attached to the base of the flash and it is triggered by the flash coming from inside the camera housing. In most cases, the trigger flash inside the housing is blocked or diverted upwards using a white card or mirror, so to avoid any backscatter particles.

The simplest flash system is one with a slave sensor in the flash head. When the camera flash is fired, the slave flash will trigger at the same time. There are even TTL slave flashes that mimic the main flash and shut off when the main flash does.

■ TIPS AND TRICKS FOR USING FLASH

Sometimes it gets complicated with new digital point & shoot cameras because they feature in internal flash and the capability of adding an auxiliary flash. Do you leave both flashes on or do you disable the built-in one? How do you fire an auxiliary flash if your housing has no sync port? Relax—we will try to answer a few of your flash questions!

If you are using a point & shoot digital camera that has a hot shoe, turn off the internal flash in the menu setup. Attach the sync cord from the camera housing to the auxiliary flash-sync port. Be sure to connect the internal portion of the plug to the camera's hot shoe and test your system before you go underwater to ensure proper camera and flash synchronization. If your camera has a hot shoe, but will not allow you to turn off the internal flash, you must find the flash's exposure compensation in the menu and set it to –2 or the lowest power setting. Otherwise, you may find that it heats up the air inside the housing over time.

Some point & shoot cameras use the internal flash to trigger an external slave flash. You may find that some use light baffles to direct the internal flash away from the scene to avoid backscatter while still triggering the slave. Other systems use a fiber optic cable attached directly to the outside of the housing that covers up the internal flash. This optic cable is then attached to an auxiliary flash and uses the output from the internal flash for its triggering device. If you set the internal flash's compensation to its lowest setting it will trigger the slave—but it may also cause it to give an underexposure. You will then have to adjust the external flash to achieve a good exposure.

■ TTL HOUSING CONTROL BOARDS

A couple of manufacturers now make special control boards inside the housing that allow the camera and flash to electronically interface.

ROC, from Light and Motion, interfaces a specific digital camera with more than a dozen different strobes. You can then manually adjust the exposure by pushing buttons to increase or decrease the flash's output.

Ikelite now offers the eTTL control boards. They enable a specific digital camera and the Ikelite flash to mimic the functions of a compatible digital flash.

■ BATTERIES

Flash units can run off AA, C cells, and proprietary battery packs. The type you use will depend on the manufacturer's determination as to what works best for that specific flash unit. The rule of thumb is that the more battery power you boast, the more flashes you will have and a faster recycle time.

For years, flash units that used AA and C cells were powered by Alkaline and Nicad batteries. The weight, power levels, and recharging problems of these batteries gave way to two new types of batteries used in digital cameras today. A few use proprietary Lithium-Ion batteries, but the bulk use the Ni-MH (Nickel Metal Hydride) rechargeable batteries. The advantage of these Ni-MH batteries is that they charge very fast and have considerably more power than their predecessors. The downside is that they can be very dangerous if they get wet. They become very hot and can explode if contained in a confined area.

For this reason, most all flash manufacturers have upgraded their flashes to include an end cap that will vent any pressure buildup inside the flash. Some manufacturers, like Sea & Sea, have gone one step further by introducing a line of flash units with a floodable battery compartment. If the flash does flood because of a defec-

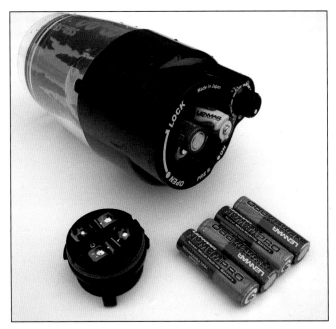

You should always have a minimum of two sets of batteries for your underwater flash so that one set is charging while you dive with the other set. The exception is if you have a dedicated flash that can high-speed charge between dives.

tive battery or excessive pressure, the flood is confined to just the battery compartment.

We recommend you have at least two full sets of flash batteries. That way you can charge one set while you're on the dive and swap them out for the next dive. This also applies to proprietary batteries. Although they do last longer, believe it or not batteries and charging systems do fail. If you spend thousands of dollars for a drive trip, why mess it up with a failed battery?

■ FLASH RECYCLE TIME

Digital photographers may wonder why, when they view their images on the monitor, some exposures vary even when nothing has changed. The reason is probably due to the recycle time of the flash. Most flash units display a ready light when it approaches a 75- to 80-percent charge. When, in the excitement of taking underwater pictures, you fire as soon as the ready light comes on, your images will be underexposed. So you make an adjustment and then take a few minutes composing your next image. Your flash actually comes up to full power during that time interval, so when you take the next shot, it will have an exposure blowout. As long as you are aware of the ready-light problem, you can adjust your images by either waiting until the flash has

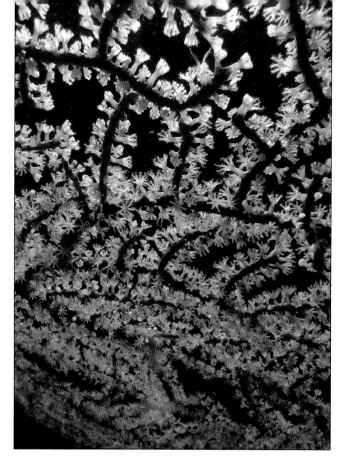

full power or adjusting your exposure when shooting fast consecutive shots.

■ SINGLE FLASH

When you use a single flash underwater, it will cast a strong shadow on the opposite side of the subject. This is fine if you use top- or backlighting and want a dramatic lighting ratio. You can reduce this harsh effect by creating a balance between the available light and the single flash. When using the manual mode, this is easily accomplished by adjusting the shutter speed until a small amount of available light fills in the shadow area (see chapter 7 on manual exposure). Although the filled area will have a bluish cast, in most cases that will be offset by the warmth of the flash on the subject.

A single flash is also a useful tool when taking close-focus, wide-angle images. In this case, the flash lights the subject close to the camera and the sun illuminates the remaining portion of the image. You will find more about taking such images in chapter 10.

You can also use a single flash on macro subjects that are very close to the camera lens. At this point, the size of the flash tube is equal to or greater than the size of the subject, so the light will wrap around the subject and you won't end up with harsh shadows. The lighting pattern in this situation will be even, much like the lighting from a fluorescent tube.

■ TWIN FLASH

One of the most popular flash configurations is a twin flash with a main flash on the left and the fill flash on the right. There are many variations for this setup. For example, housings that support two sync cords will have one for each flash, while single-port housing will have to use a Y-flash connector to operate both flash systems.

In most cases, the twin-flash system will be a matched pair with ratio lighting controlled by distance, diffusers, or power levels on the back of the flash unit. Generally speaking, the fill flash will be the weaker flash close to the camera, while the main flash will have more power and be used at various angles to the subject in the scene.

Another configuration with twin flash systems is one large flash attached to the camera via a sync cable and a smaller slave flash that acts as a fill light. We like to keep

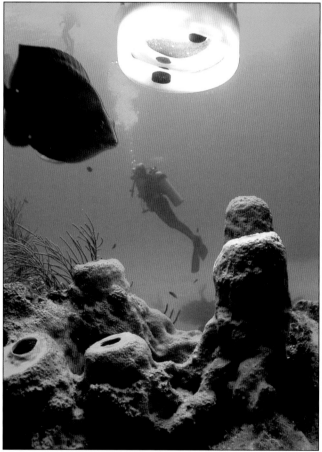

A single flash can create some very dynamic lighting when it is moved around to different angles.

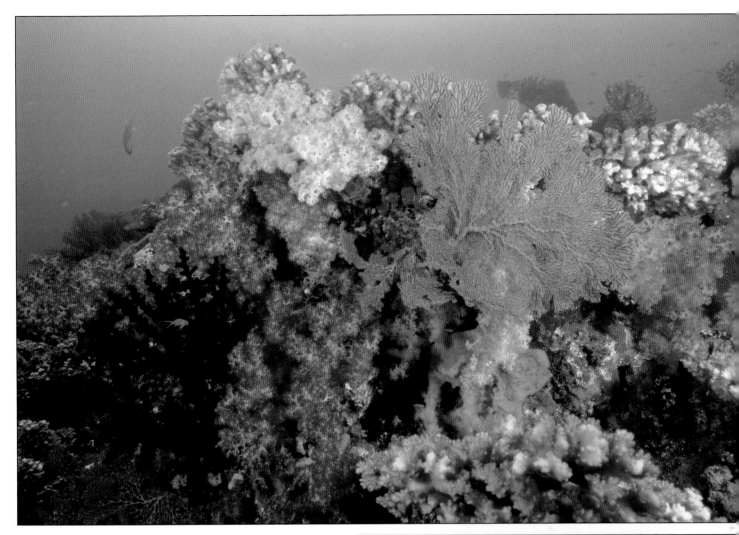

ABOVE AND RIGHT—This Fijian soft coral image was taken with a digital SLR housing, super-wide lens, and two flashes extended out on long arms.

the slave flash smaller so that it does not overpower the main flash in the scene.

◼ WIDE-ANGLE FLASH

If you are shooting wide-angle images with flash, you will need a large flash with a very wide beam angle designed for wide-angle photography. Most flash units today will have a specification sheet telling you how wide the beam angle is and what lens focal length it will cover. If you find that your flash coverage is close with some falloff, it may be a simple matter of placing a diffuser over the flash head. Most flash units come with a diffuser, and it should be used for super-wide shots. The diffuser will decrease some of the light output, but the evenness of the lighting will be worth it.

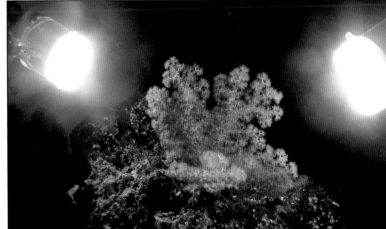

One way to ensure that you cover the scene is to use two wide-angle flash units evenly spread on each side of the camera. The wider the camera lens, the more you will point the flash heads away from the center of the scene. This is especially true if you have particulate matter (backscatter) floating through the water. You can test your twin-flash coverage ahead of time by pointing

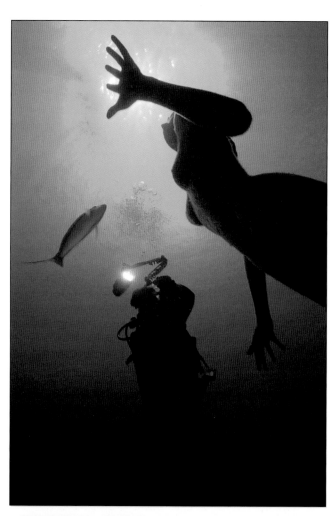

the system at a blank wall and viewing the pattern on the LCD viewer on the back of the camera. When the wall image is evenly lit, make note of the angle of the flash units so that you can approximate it underwater.

■ SLAVE FLASH

When taking a picture of another photographer, it has always been popular to have your flash trigger theirs so it appears as if they are really taking an image. For many years this concept worked very well with film systems, but digital now presents a new problem. Most digital cameras do not have the ability to capture the full exposure range of a bright flash firing into the camera lens and still maintain subject detail elsewhere in the scene. Added to the problem is the fact that digital camera sensors are very sensitive, so even the smallest amount of direct flash output may be too much. We have had

LEFT—This famous statue in front of Sunset House in the Cayman Islands is the perfect setting for this slave-flash test. Set the digital camera to slave and a low power setting, so that when the main camera's flash triggers the slave it will not overexpose the scene. BELOW—Because the diver's flash was fired remotely by slave, it appears as if she is actually taking this image of two angelfish.

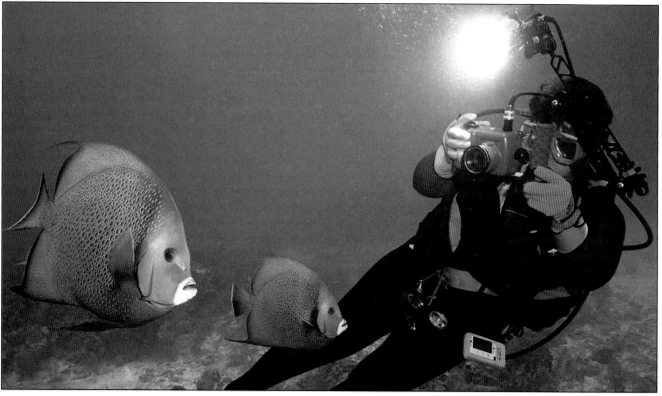

some success by setting the digital camera to ISO 100 at f/8, and setting the slave flash to $\frac{1}{16}$ power. We have also found that if you point the slave flash at a slight angle to the camera and avoid the straight-on approach, you will get better results.

■ FLASH ARMS AND CAMERA TRAYS

You can find almost any configuration available for mounting your camera and flash. There are trays, trays with arms, flexible arms, and rigid bars. Those with rigid arms come in sections that can be joined together using ball joints. Ultralight Control Systems (www.ulcs .com) offers a wide variety of arms and trays designed for the underwater photographer. They even have a tray that rotates, allowing you to take either vertical or horizontal images with the click of button.

If you are planning to take macro photos, then you will need shorter arms to enable the light to illuminate your small subject. When taking general reef shots, a longer arm is necessary to evenly illuminate the scene.

For wide-angle photos, we recommend that you set up your flash-arm system so that each side is made up of at least two sections. That way if you want a flash unit close, you can fold up one or both sections. If you want to extend the flashes, just lock all the arms in a straight line and they will extend as far as possible from the camera. Another advantage is that the arms can be folded compactly to the camera as you enter and exit the water. This helps make transporting a large camera system a little bit easier.

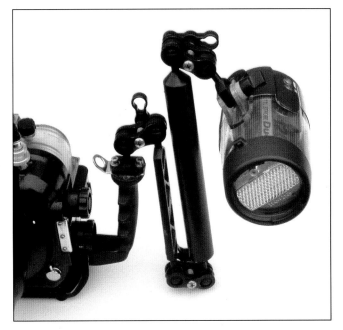

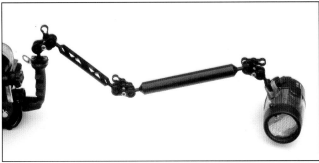

When using a digital SLR system and extended flash arms, you should fold the arms up tight to the camera body before you make the dive. Once underwater, you can then extend the arms to the position that provides the best lighting.

10. Wide-Angle Photography

The art of wide-angle photography requires a unique blend of high-quality lens optics, a good working knowledge of flash-fill exposure, an eye for good composition, and just the right subject matter. When we used the old silver process of film, the Nikonos and 15mm lens was the king of wide angle. Its optics were suburb, the angle of coverage extreme, and best of all, the Nikonos camera system was compact. Today it is still an incredible wide-angle system and hard to beat. But hang on! There's another kid on the block, and he's knocking at your door.

■ DIGITAL LENS CONFIGURATIONS

Behind door number one we have the digital CCD SLR. The CCD SLR cameras don't cover the exact same area as 35mm film; in fact, you must multiply the focal length of your lens by approximately 1.5 to determine the effective focal length. This means that your 20mm is around 30mm, and your 14mm is now a 21mm—which drastically reduces the effect of the super-wide-angle lenses. The only real way to match the image range of the Nikonos 15 with a CCD SLR is to use a fisheye lens in a very large dome port. While we

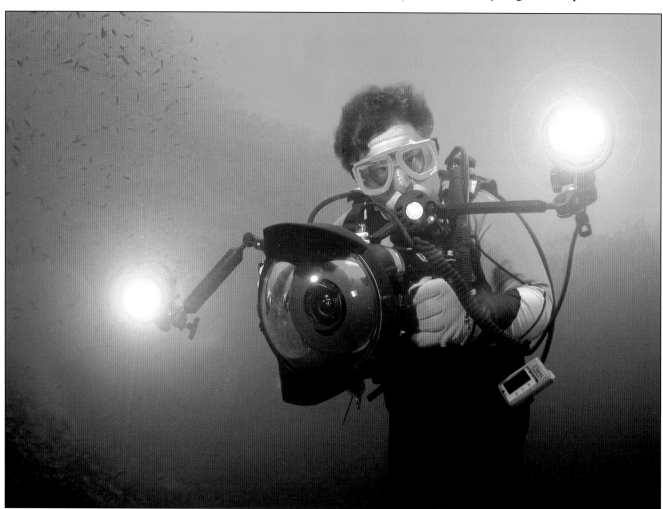

Sue is shown here with a digital SLR housing, super-wide dome port, and twin flash. With this system, she can get close to the subject, reduce the water column, and get some very dramatic wide-angle images.

have seen a few of these configurations, we find the image distortion and the bulkiness of the system a deterrent.

Behind door number two we have the CMOS SLR. We have seen a couple that fill the full-frame 35mm format, but their limited availability, added expense, and bulkiness is still too much for the average underwater photographer.

That leaves us at door number three where we find the digital point & shoot camera. Since most digital point & shoot cameras have a single, permanent zoom lens, the only way to extend the angle of coverage is with an accessory lens.

■ WET LENSES

Fortunately, the solution came early in the development of small underwater housings and it evolved into accessory lenses that could be attached while underwater. The wet-lens concept caught on quickly and led to a wide selection of both macro and wide-angle lenses that can be adapted to all different levels of underwater housings. Sea & Sea leads the pack by offering a wide variety of lens adapters that slide over the front lens of many compact camera housings. They also came up with the great idea of incorporating their accessory lenses, which were originally designed for the MX-10 and MotorMarine II line of film cameras. These accessory lenses just bayonet mount onto the front of their popular line of digital-camera housings.

The popularity of this concept has expanded to create a new breed of high-quality, super-wide wet lenses. These lenses use 67mm threads to fit on housings from Light & Motion, Olympus, and Ikelite. They feature a very wide angle of view, only a slight amount of distortion, and are very sharp. We feel that many of these combinations are the digital equivalent of the esteemed Nikonos 15mm.

The downside is that some of these lenses weigh a lot and must be factored as part of your weight-belt allocation. Thankfully, accessory manufacturers have recently added lens caddies that attach to strobes arms so you can take the lens off and shoot macro. If you're one of those photographers who wished they could take all types of images with just one camera, then this combination might just be your answer.

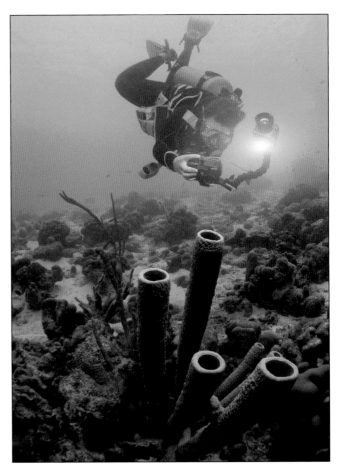

This is our daughter Kristy on her first underwater photography trip to Bonaire. She used this digital point & shoot with its built-in zoom lens to capture the sponge in the foreground.

A bonus to using the point & shoot camera for super-wide images is that, because the chip is so small, the depth of field can be almost four times greater than that achieve with film cameras at the same f/stop. This means that f/8 on a point & shoot camera is equivalent to f/16 on a film camera. An additional benefit is that this system is almost as compact as the Nikonos and 15mm lens.

Don't get us wrong, the SLR and wide-angle lens with a dome port does a great job, too. It's still the answer if you already own the necessary lenses and SLR camera. You just need to be aware that is it a bulky configuration. If, however, you haven't yet made the camera and lens investment, we recommend that you go the direction of a point & shoot camera with a wet lens.

■ REDUCING THE WATER COLUMN

A big advantage of the wide-angle lens is that you can get closer to large objects underwater. You can still keep

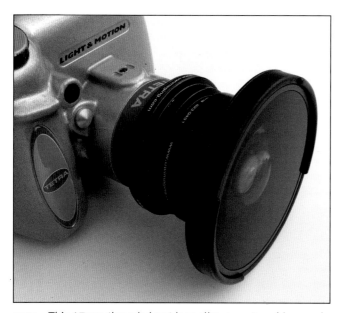

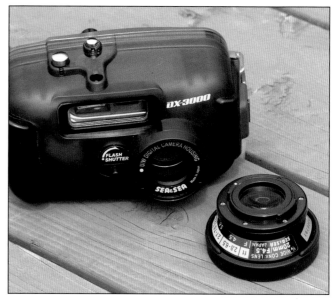

LEFT—This 67mm threaded wet lens allows you to achieve underwater wide-angle images that resemble those taken with a Nikonos and 15mm lens. These lenses can be attached underwater and several manufacturers now make them for a variety of point & shoot housings. RIGHT—The bayonet-mounted wide-angle wet lens that was originally used for the MX-10 film camera can now be used on several digital Sea & Sea camera systems.

them in the frame, yet the water between the camera and subject is reduced. Because this water column is reduced, the image sharpness increases and the backscatter is minimized. You also have more control with your lighting, since you can now move your flash from side to side and behind the subject.

■ CAMERA ANGLES

The wide-angle lens can be one of the most creative tools for underwater photography when used to its maximum potential. One popular technique is to vary your camera angle by shooting the subject from a high, medium, and low angle. This isn't a new technique, as wide-angle photographers have been shooting at weird angles underwater for some time. The difference today is that reef awareness is a major concern, and we have to be very careful not to get too close to the fragile environment around us. This makes it more difficult to get down under sea fans and soft corals that are close to the reef.

With a compact digital point & shoot camera and a wet lens, you can operate the entire system with one hand. That makes it easy to place the camera at varying angles without having to be directly behind the camera to take the shot. In some cases, you can even see the LCD from an angle and compose your image. Other

times you will have to guess at the correct angle, turn the camera for a preview, adjust the angle and try again. You may find that you rarely have to be directly behind the LCD viewer to get some great camera angles.

To really understand how a point of view can change your perception of a subject, we suggest that you try photographing a stationary subject while varying your view. For example, find a large sponge and shoot straight down first, and continue shooting as you move to various angles. You may be surprised to find new camera angles you haven't used before.

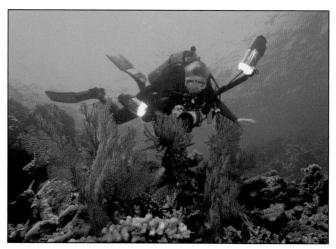

When shooting with a bulky wide-angle system, it is critical that you have good buoyancy so you can protect the reef as you move into unique camera positions.

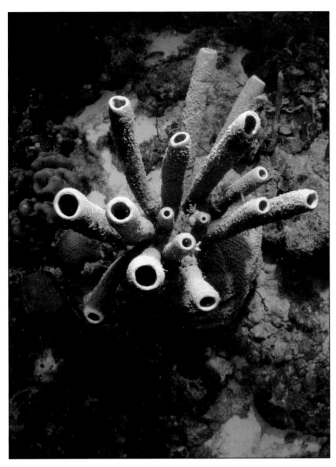

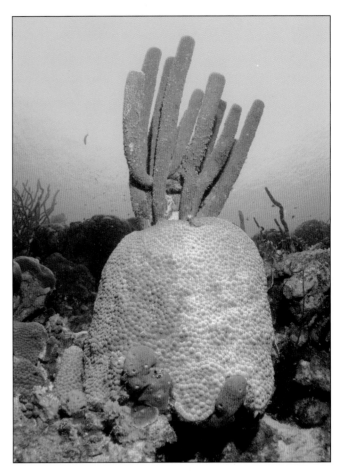

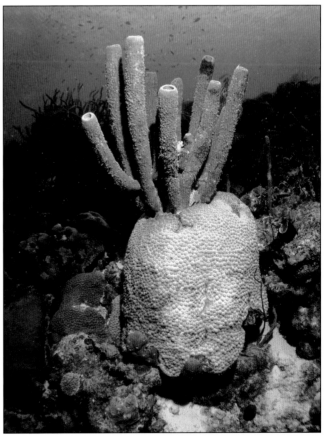

When shooting with a wide-angle system, you should move around the subject taking images from all different angles. You may be surprised to find unique camera angles that result in better images.

■ PERSPECTIVE APPLICATIONS

Another creative aspect of wide-angle photography is that you can create increased perspective by shooting small objects close to the lens and larger objects in the background. In most cases, the depth of field with the super-wide wet lenses will be enough to keep both objects in focus. The end result is that the close, small objects will appear almost as big as the distant, larger object—or sometimes even bigger.

With digital point & shoot cameras you can take this exaggeration even further by setting the camera into the close-up mode. When this happens, your lens should be able to focus as close as one inch away and still carry depth of field to several feet away. In order for this wide-angle close-up technique to really work, you need to consider two other factors to get the best shot.

First, the focus point on most point & shoot cameras will be directly in the center of the image. If you

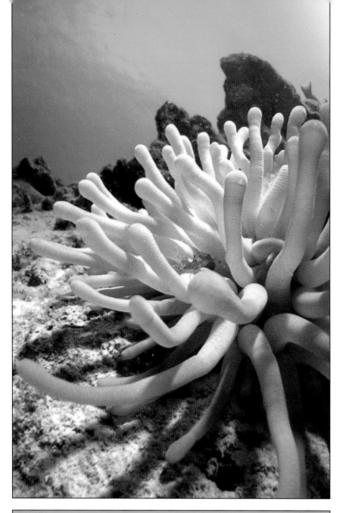

shoot a vertical image with the small object at the bottom and the large at the top, the camera will focus half way in between leaving the close object out of focus. You can rectify this by going into the focus menu and setting it to manual. This will allow you to toggle the focus point to the bottom of the screen, allowing for maximum depth of field.

The second problem you will encounter is incorrect lighting. You are trying to evenly light a subject that is only one inch away yet uniformly light the rest of the distant scene. This feat of lighting magic can be accomplished by placing the flash on a very long arm high over the scene and setting the ISO speed to 400. Point the flash toward the middle of the scene so that, when it fires, it will feather the light from the close object to the distance ones. This may sound complicated, but once you give it a try and keep reviewing your efforts in the LCD finder, you will find that is can easily be done even with a single flash. You can also adjust your shutter speed so that the available light and flash blend together.

■ SHIPWRECKS

You have two choices when shooting wide-angle images of shipwrecks: flash and no flash. If the visibility is extremely low or there is a lot of particulate in the water, you will want the flash off and the widest lens possible. If you want a spot of color in the image, have another diver carrying a bright flashlight in the scene. The low visibility will produce backscatter in front of the flashlight and create a great effect—you'll be the envy of the Hollywood special-effects guys!

If you do have some water clarity, you can place your flash on a long arm so that it can light colorful objects in the foreground. Since you will be dealing with more particulate than normal, we recommend that

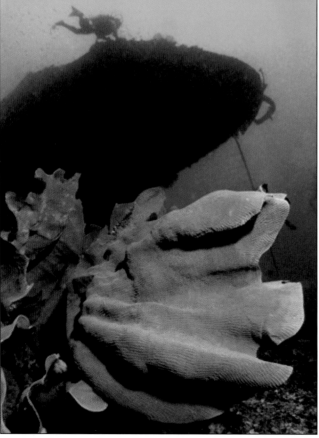

TOP—This close-focus wide-angle image of a sea anemone was taken with a digital point & shoot camera and a super-wide wet lens attachment. The lens was placed less than an inch away from the subject and the flash was placed on a long arm to spread the light a couple of feet away. BOTTOM—This wide-angle image of a shipwreck was taken with a digital point & shoot camera and a wet lens. The flash was extended on a long Ultralight arm so the flash pointed towards the colorful subject in the foreground.

you reduce the shutter speed to a level where the background light is almost equal to the flash exposure. This blending of light will keep the backscatter effect to a minimum. See more on backscatter in chapter 14.

■ WORKING WITH MODELS

One of the most difficult types of wide-angle photography is when you work with models. The problem is not with the photo equipment, but rather the lack of communication between photographer and model. If you want to attempt this sophisticated type of photography, you should first decide on some clear-cut hand signals. Then work in as shallow water as possible, and use the custom white balance. If you decide to use flash, be sure to use flash fill if possible and balance the background

RIGHT—This self portrait of Jack was taken in San Salvador, Bahamas using a Nikonos 5 and a Light Handle flash system (Patented by Jack and Sue Drafahl). BELOW—Our trusty model, Wanda, is shown swimming with a school of fish in San Salvador, Bahamas. This early image was taken with a Nikonos camera and a 15mm lens.

exposure using the shutter speed. Finally, don't try to do too much on a single dive. Work on just a couple of shots per dive, taking as many variations as possible.

■ SELF PORTRAIT

Many years ago we developed a technique we dubbed "Self Portrait with a 15." When the water was really dirty, we found that two divers in close proximity often stirred up the bottom too much for photography. These

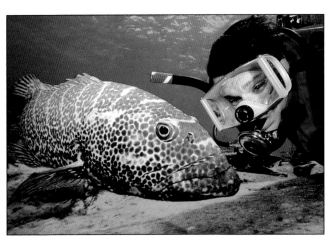

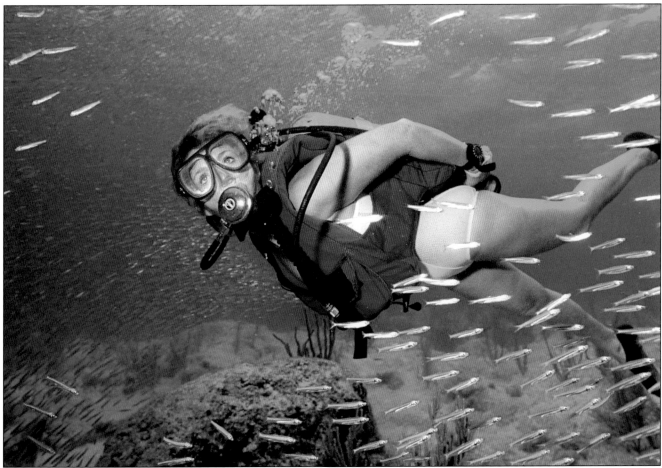

self-portraits required a compact camera system that was balanced so that you could hold it all with one hand. Using the Nikonos and a 15mm lens, we found that it only required one person to both shoot and pose. Best of all it was easy. Just extend your arm, holding the camera lens looking back toward yourself and place an animal between you and the camera. Use the reflection on the front of the lens to compose the image and press the shutter for your self portrait.

The compact digital cameras with some of the wider accessory lenses are also compact enough for self portraits. The difference is that, after each shot, you can turn the system around and see what modifications are necessary to make the shot even better.

■ PANORAMIC REEF IMAGES

The grand panorama is one of the most difficult images to accomplish using a wide-angle system. This is the type of image you see in coffee table books where the lighting is perfect, soft corals of every color flourish from left to right, fish abound, and everything is photographically perfect. Wow!

The first step is to find a reef worthy of a grand panorama. The water has to be very clear and toward the shallow end of the ocean. To get the best flash illumination, use a matched set of powerful, wide-angle flashes on long arms. The flash heads should be set to evenly feather the light, right out to the edges without any falloff. The lighting ratio should be slight, so that you can barely tell a flash was used but the reef still has vibrant color.

What we have described here is an image that many photographers may never achieve in a lifetime, but is a worthy goal for which to strive. If you do find a suitable reef, we recommend that you spend the entire dive if necessary to get the shot. Work with exposure variations, various angles, and framing techniques until you can surface and say "I've got it!" . . . unless you are about to run out of air.

An alternate method for creating a panoramic reef image is to photograph the reef in sections, then stitch it together using panorama software. For best results, you need to have even lighting in each section and overlap each image by about 50 percent. You will also have to move parallel to the reef as you shoot each part. If you were to take all the images from just one point, it would give you a fisheye effect, and that is not as effective. To simplify the stitching process, you should set your camera to manual exposure and use the same exposure for all the panoramic parts.

FACING PAGE—This pristine Fijian reef covered with soft coral was photographed with a digital SLR housing, super-wide-angle lens, and two large flash units extended on Ultralight flash arms. BELOW—This is a composite image created from eight overlapping photographs that were stitched together using special editing software.

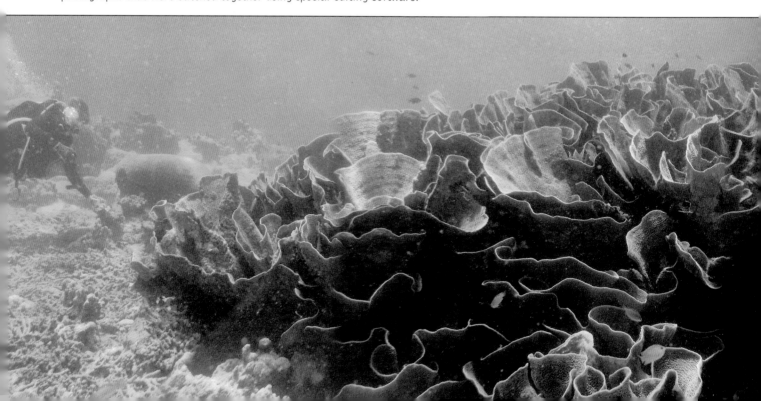

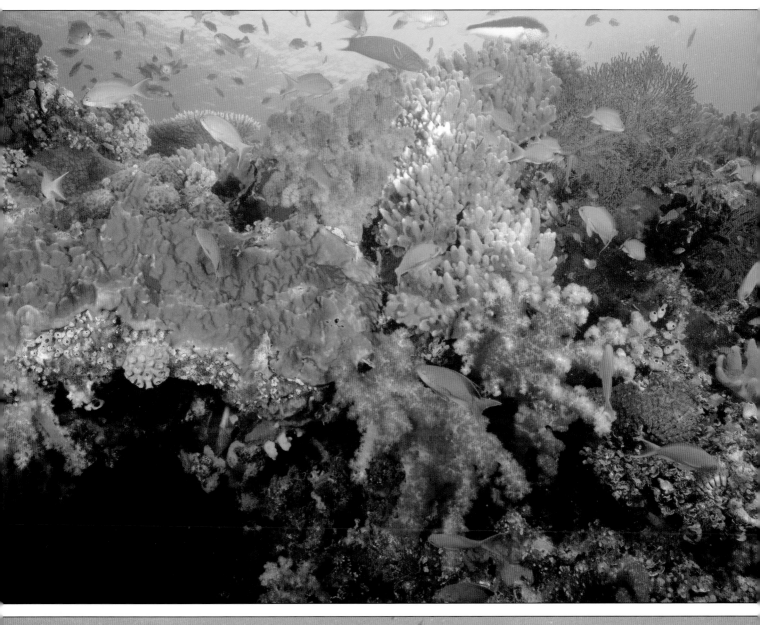

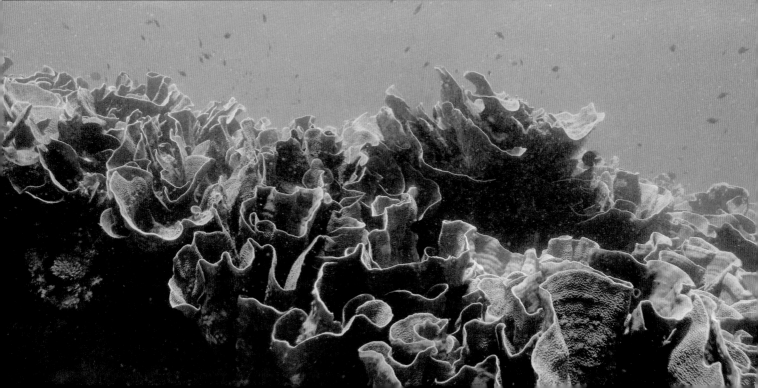

11. Fish Photography

Of all the subjects in underwater photography, fish are one of the most popular—but also one of the most difficult. Most fish are somewhat skittish and shy away from the underwater camera lens. Topside, it's easy to photograph animals from a distance, since you can just use a telephoto lens and the problem is solved. Underwater, it's a different story. If you increase your camera-to-subject distance in order to minimize the fear impact, other problems occur. For instance, the increased distance increases the water column, which in turn decreases sharpness, contrast, color, and overall image quality. But don't despair! There are several ways to address the solution. Since there is enough difference in solutions between film shooters and digital, we will address them each separately.

■ FILM PHOTOGRAPHY

Lens and Camera Choices. The solution for film photographers is easy. To get the best fish pictures on film, you will need an SLR housed system with a 100–105mm short telephoto macro lens. This is a good choice because it provides a safe distance for taking images of shy creatures. These macro lenses are designed to be very sharp at very small apertures, and the focus ranges from infinity down to a 1:1 magnification ratio. You can limit the focus range on most of

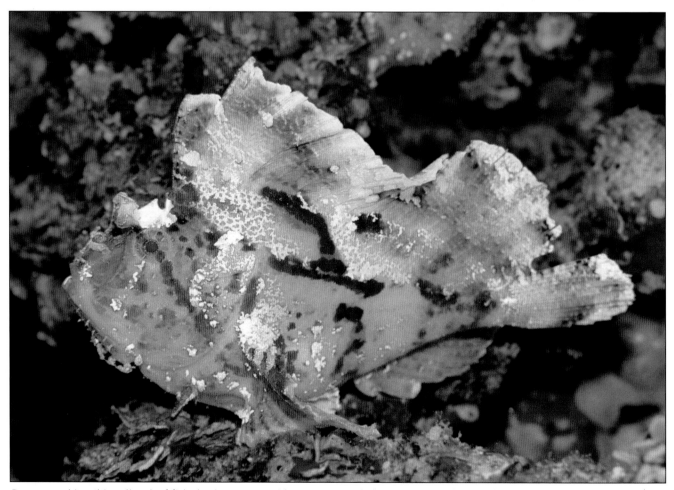

By approaching this yellow leaf fish slowly, we were able to get several close-up views using a Nikon 8008 and color negative film.

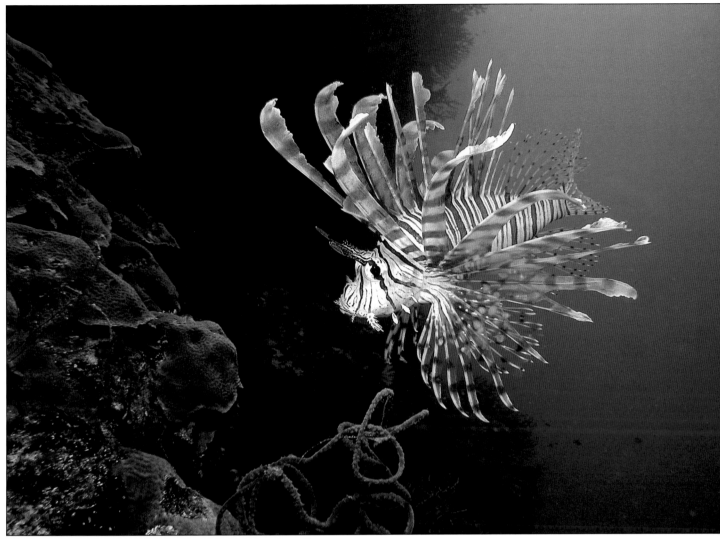

This lion fish in Fiji was photographed using a point & shoot digital camera and a single flash.

these lenses so that you don't have that constant searching throughout the entire focus range.

The 50–60mm SLR macro lens is very popular for land photography, but you may find that you have to get too close to the fish to get a decent magnification. We have tried it many times and always get very frustrated when the fish scoots away just as we start to get up close and personal. We find that we always head back to the 105mm macro lens for our best shots. Another big advantage to the 105mm macro is that you can still continue shooting other macro subjects like nudibranchs when the fish won't cooperate.

Point & shoot and amphibious film cameras generally do not have an adequate viewing or focusing system for getting good fish images. There are a few systems that have wands, close-up kits, or framers, but there is

still a lot of guesswork involved in getting just a few good shots.

Film Choices. Slide-film shooters will generally find that ISO 100 film pushed to ISO 200 works the best for fish photography, since the pushed film will add contrast and saturation to your images. The grain will also be increased, but if you plan on scanning your images, you can use the new grain-reduction technology called Digital GEM (from Kodak [www.asf.com]) to help negate this issue.

We have found the best film for fish photography is color negative film in the ISO 400–800 range. In the last few years, there has been extensive research conducted on these negative film stocks and they really work well, especially underwater. The big advantage, of course, is that the higher ISO provides more control

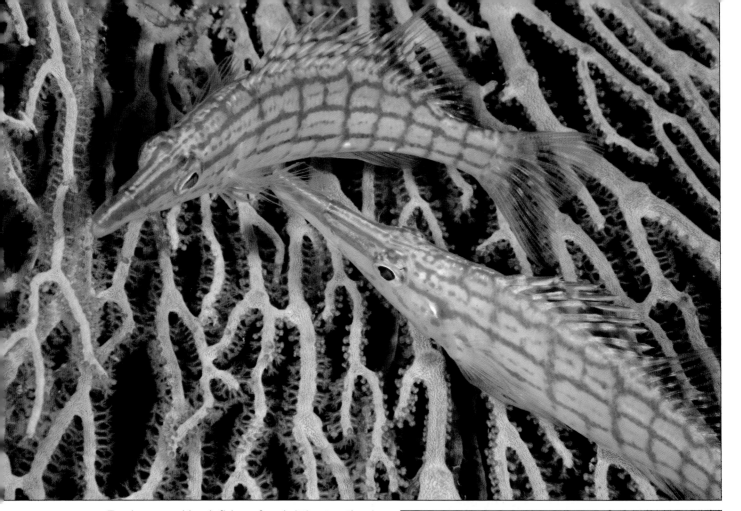

ABOVE—Two long-nosed hawk fish we found sitting together in the Solomon Islands and photographed with a digital SLR housing and a twin-flash system. RIGHT—A typical digital SLR fish camera system with a long lens port and twin flashes.

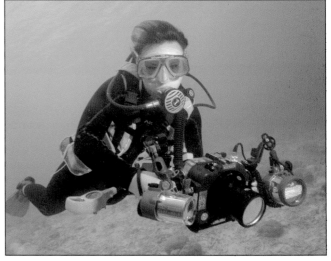

over f/stop and the action-stopping power of the shutter speed. It also allows for flexibility in flash size, which is necessary for obtaining good exposures from three to four feet away. Again, any grain-related problems from shooting on color negative films are negated with grain-reduction technologies like Digital GEM.

■ DIGITAL PHOTOGRAPHY

The main difference between film and digital cameras in regard to taking fish photos is that you can easily use both digital point & shoot and digital SLR cameras. Essentially, almost all digital cameras underwater have the potential for taking great fish pictures.

Point & Shoot. The very fact that point & shoot cameras have an LCD viewfinder that shows you exactly what you are shooting gives them the same advantage as the film SLR cameras. The key to their success is that they have both zoom lens and close-up functions. Since many of the point & shoot cameras have the same effective focal length as the 105mm on a film SLR camera, they can capture fish almost as easily. Note that we said *almost*.

The problem with digital point & shoot cameras is the shutter delay. The camera must switch between preview screen to the viewing screen and still activate the autofocus system. All those functions take time and the camera must wait until they are accomplished. Because of this delay, you may find that the fish is gone before the shutter actually fires. Not to worry, though. This problem is slowly going away and newer breeds of point & shoot cameras have less and less delay.

If you become frustrated trying to take pictures of fish because of this shutter delay, don't completely blame the technology. If you were to hand a digital point & shoot camera to a seasoned video photographer, they would have no difficulty shooting fish pictures, as they know how to pan with their subjects. All you need to do is to pan the camera along with the action of the fish and fire the shutter as you follow through in order to get some great shots. Don't get impatient—it takes some practice, but in time you will achieve results. Remember back in chapter 6, we stated that you needed to practice on land with moving objects like your children or pets to help improve your panning skills? It's important to keep honing your skills—including panning—between dive trips.

Digital SLR. You would assume that shooting with a digital SLR camera would parallel the film shooter,

right? That would be the case if your digital SLR camera used a CMOS chip the same frame size as a film. Instead the CCD chip magnifies the image by 1.4 to 1.5 times, which means that your 100-105mm lens now becomes a 150–160mm lens. Generally, with this lens you would have to move too far back to photograph fish and the increased water column would reduce the quality of your image. It is a great lens for photographing fish parts, fish cleaning stations, or extreme macro images, but it is difficult to photograph an entire fish. You would need to go back to the 50–60mm macro lens, which with digital magnification would become a 75–90mm, a much better lens choice for fish photography. If you really want to cover the field, we recommend that you have a port system that will accommodate either lens, so you can use both, depending on the situation.

There is another big advantage to photographing fish with digital SLR cameras. Since the water column is greater, there normally would be a loss of color, saturation, and contrast with a film camera. The more ad-

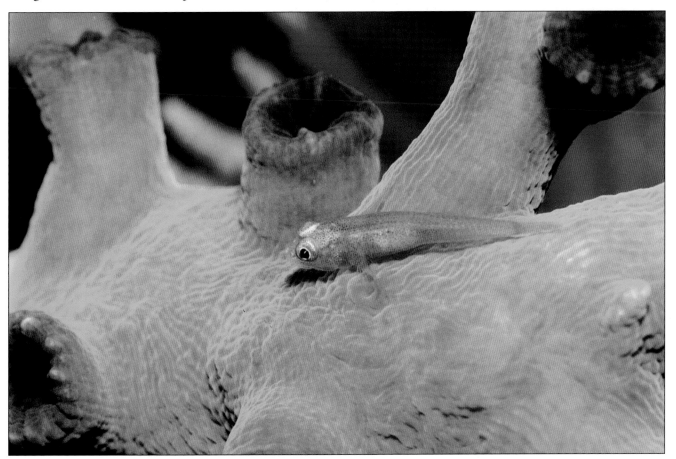

A macro lens set to 1:1 magnification on a digital SLR camera was used to document this tiny fish.

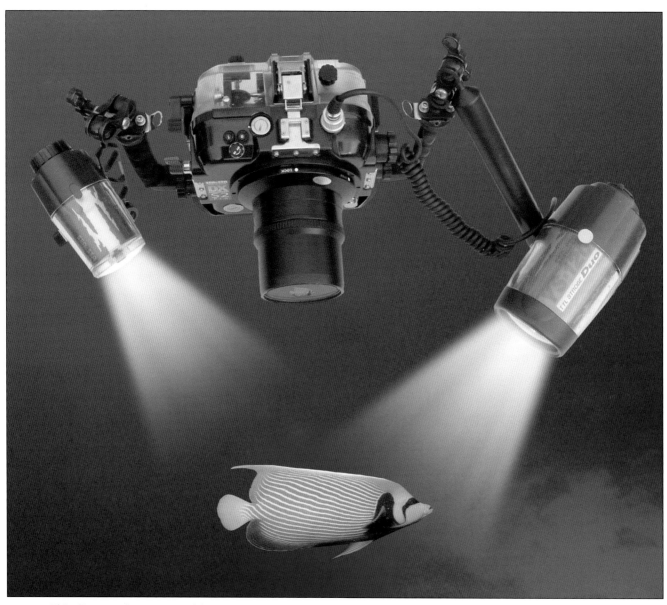

ABOVE—This diagram shows a typical lighting setup for fish photography. The main light on the right should be towards the fish's head, while the fill light should light the tail. FACING PAGE—We slowly approached this crocodile fish in the Solomon Islands, taking a picture every few inches until we had just the eye in the finder.

vanced digital SLR cameras today have contrast and saturation controls than can help negate many of these problems.

Since digital camera noise at ISO 400–800 is considerably less than film at the same ISO speed, you can use these speeds as your norm when photographing fish. This increased speed provides more control over your background exposure, depth of field, and exposure. There is also technology designed to reduce the small amount of digital noise that appears at the higher ISO speeds. One of the best is called Dfine from nik Multimedia (www.nikmultimedia.com).

■ FLASH CONSIDERATIONS

When using a digital SLR system, the flash system we find works best is a large main light with a narrow beam and a very small flash for fill light. With most large flash units today, you can narrow the beam merely by taking off the flash diffuser. The reason you need a narrow flash beam is that you only want to light the fish. If you light the rest of the water column between the camera lens and the fish, you will get backscatter.

Since there is some distance between the camera lens and the fish, you will want to place the flash out on an arm, some distance from the camera. The real trick

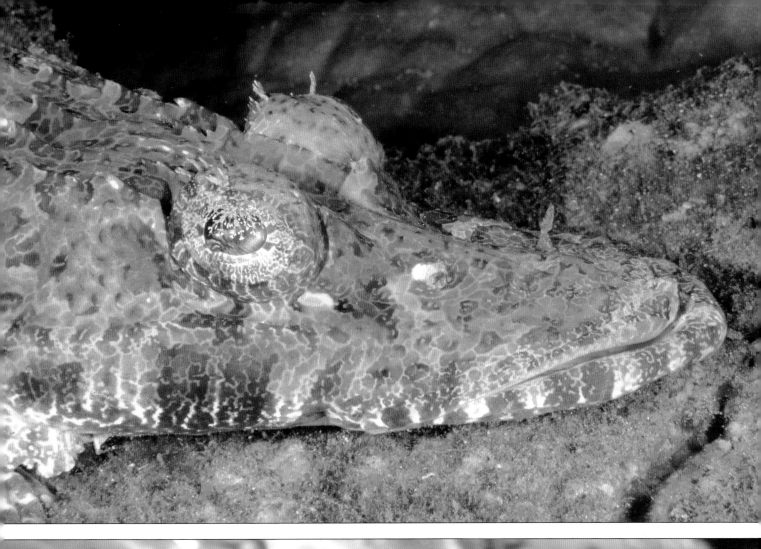
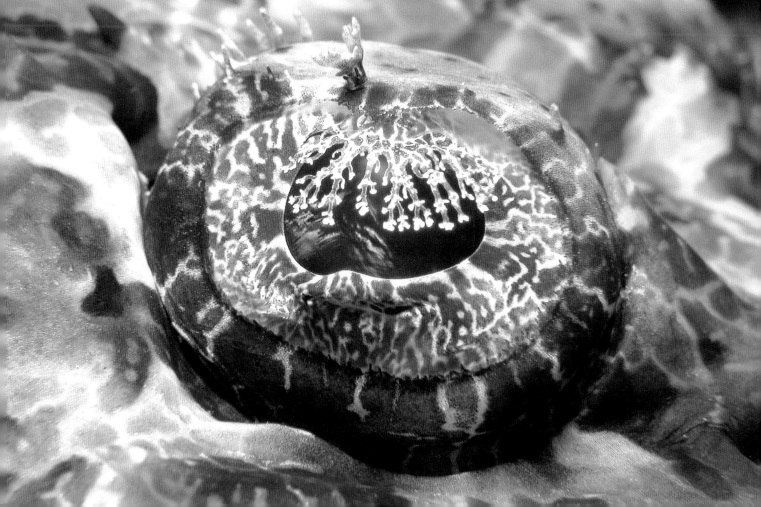

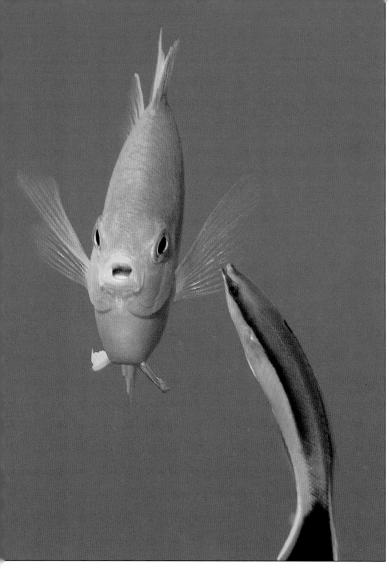
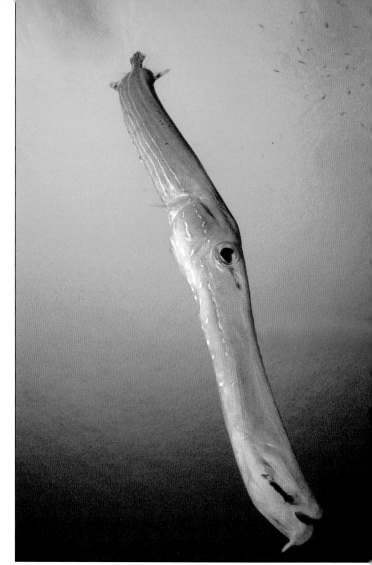

LEFT—In order to capture this image, we spent most of an entire dive at this single cleaning station. A digital SLR camera with a 105mm macro lens and twin flashes were used in order to maintain a safe shooting distance from the fish. RIGHT—A very curious yellow trumpet fish looks at his or her reflection in the super-wide wet lens. A single flash on a long arm was used to evenly light the fish.

here is proper aiming of the flash so that it lights the position where the fish is in focus. The easiest way we have found to make this adjustment is to turn the camera and flash around and use your face mask as the correct fish placement. You can then adjust the flash so that it only illuminates your face. This distance should work well when you finally give it a try with the fish.

The smaller flash should be placed on the opposite side of the housing and be set to half of the main flash's power or less. If the water is very dirty, you may have to turn this fill flash off completely and depend solely on the single narrow beam flash. This twin-flash system works well to negate any shadows falling on the background, but when photographing fish in open water this isn't generally a problem.

Digital point & shoot cameras are a little more limited on flash configurations since most use an internal flash or a slave-fired external flash. With this type of camera, we generally use just the one external slave flash and work the flash angles to minimize the shadows on the background. The best solution is if you have a point & shoot camera that has a hot shoe and sync port. With this system, you can use the sync flash alone or in conjunction with another slaved flash, just like the SLR shooters.

◼ TECHNIQUES FOR PHOTOGRAPHING FISH

Part of the technique of getting a good picture goes way beyond the equipment. You need to understand the reef realm. Taking the time to study animal behavior will make it easier to estimate an animal's next direction. Move slowly so the fish have time to adjust to your presence. Start with a distant shot, and then a second, or third. If your fish is happy and hangs around, then move in for a closer shot. Get the fish used to your flash before moving in to a new magnification. If you keep your subject happy, you may even end up with a fish eye shot.

Spend time looking around the reef and you will see that many of the animals have specific routes they travel time and time again. These swimming fish often require the repetition approach—shooting again and again as the fish swim back and forth. Don't get discouraged, as eventually you'll get the shot you want.

One of our favorite subjects to photograph is fish cleaning stations. This is an area on the reef where fish of all shapes and sizes come together to have their bodies and gills cleaned by cleaner shrimp or fish. It may require extreme patience and often most of a dive to get some good fish-cleaning pictures. The higher ISO speeds make it easier to keep your distance and still stop the action. At first, the fish cleaning station will be in chaos as they become accustomed to a diver hovering next to their operation. In time, however, they forget you are there—and that's when you get your best shots.

We have found over the years that the one thing animals fear the most is other animals' eyes. Fish even have eye spots to lure or hide from predators. If you hide your eyes from their view, you have a much better chance of approaching them and taking some great shots. When you view the animal from behind your camera eyepiece, your eyes are blocked from the fish's view. The odds are greater that you can now get closer to the fish than you think. You may laugh at the concept, but before you do, try it a few times. Approach a fish with your eyes behind the camera, and then move the camera so the fish can see your eyes. There's a good chance it will quickly swim away, proving our point.

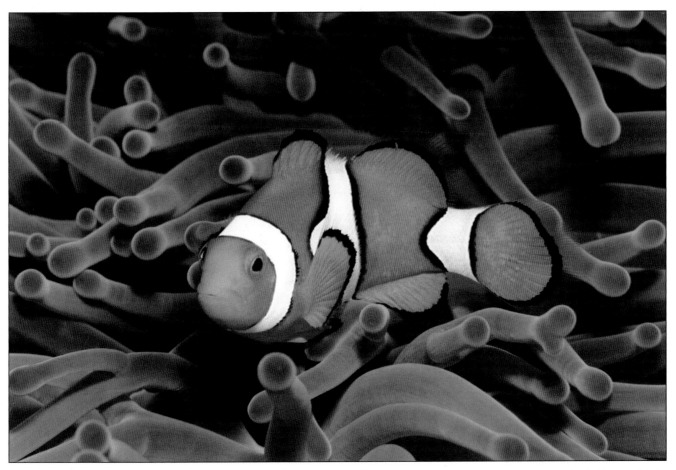

Move slowly so the fish have time to adjust to your presence. Start with a distant shot, and then a second, or third. If your fish is happy and hangs around, then move in for a closer shot.

12. Close-Up Photography

nother popular type of underwater photography is taking pictures of little critters. There is something exhilarating when you discover something as simple as a nudibranch that is smaller than your little finger. Your quest for subject matter forces you to slow down as you cruise the reef and you will quickly find that the abundance of animal life that inhabits the inner reef structure is astronomical. Best of all, the equipment needed for this type of photography is nominal and the system is compact. The distance between the lens and your subject is minimal, which reduces the water column and allows for clearer photos.

This close proximity also gives you plenty of light from your flash. Once you zero in your close-up photo system, you will be amazed at the high percentage of good photos you will be able to expose in one short dive.

■ CLOSE-UP TERMINOLOGY

There has been much confusion as to what constitutes a close-up image. How does that compare with a macro image, or a super-macro image? The problem is that each camera manufacturer uses these terms to best fit their own equipment, without any regard to their competitor's terminology or specifications.

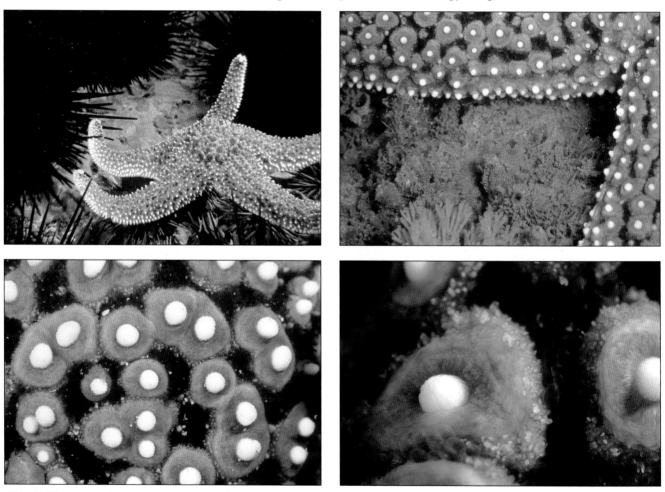

This California starfish was photographed at different close-up magnifications. TOP LEFT—1:10 magnification. TOP RIGHT—1:4 magnification. BOTTOM LEFT—1:2 magnification. BOTTOM RIGHT—1:1 magnification.

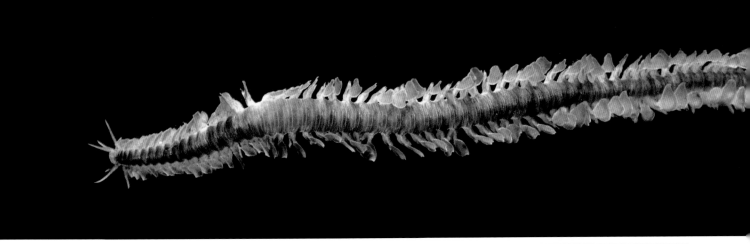

ABOVE—Night photographs can provide some unique animals, like this worm photographed on slide film with a Nikonos 1:3 framer and a single flash. RIGHT—Bayonet-mounted framers were originally designed for film cameras but have been adapted to digital cameras that feature the same bayonet-mounting system.

As avid shooters of close-up photography both topside and underwater for 35 years, we have seen a general trend of terms that seem to fit most systems both topside and underwater. We see close-up photography starting at magnification ratios of 1:10 and continuing down to 1:4. The 1:10 ratio means the actual subject size is 10 times larger than the captured image size on sensitized medium whether it be film, CCD, or CMOS. This means that a 360mm wide subject would be 36mm wide on the sensitized medium for a 1:10 magnification ratio. The 1:4 ratio would have a subject 144mm across that is reduced down to 36mm on the sensitized medium. Are you confused yet?

We see most macro systems starting where close-up left off at 1:4 magnification and going down to 1:1 in size. At this 1:1 size, the subject and the captured image on the sensitized medium would be exactly the same size. Super-macro images are usually considered larger-than-life-size images and range from 1:1 to 10:1 magnification. A 2:1 magnification ratio means that the subject is magnified two times larger on the capture medium than the actual subject's size. Most close-up photographers agree that magnifications above 10:1 are considered to be in the microscope range and beyond the capabilities of most underwater photographers.

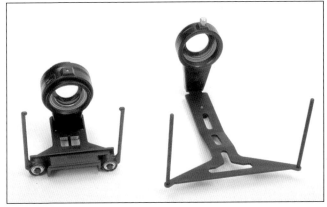

■ CLOSE-UP EQUIPMENT

We consider film shooters an integral part of the digital world since they scan their images, so we will first look at their close-up equipment.

Extension Tubes and Framers. One of the oldest, most compact, and easiest to use close-up systems is commonly called the macro framer system. The first to come on the market was the extension tube and framer for the amphibious Nikonos film camera. To set up this system, you inserted an extension tube between the camera body and its lens. This changed the optics of the camera lens so that it could shoot much closer. The extension tubes came in different sizes, and the longer the extension tube, the closer you could shoot to the subject. Since this made framing and focus extremely critical, a framing device was attached to the bottom of the extension tube so that you could frame, focus, and center the subject.

In more recent times a wet version of the extension tube and framer was developed, allowing you to attach and remove the close-up system underwater. The extension tube was replaced with a high-magnification close-up lens, and the framer concept prevailed. These systems are very popular with the Sea & Sea, Sealife, and Bonica film and digital camera systems today.

All these extension tubes and framers range from 1:10 down to 2:1 magnification depending on their configuration. There are some custom systems on the market for magnifications beyond 2:1, but they are very difficult to use.

SLR Macro Lenses. Film and digital SLR cameras have the added advantage of various lens options for close-up photography. You can achieve some outstanding close-up images using any of the different macro lenses that range in focal length from 50mm to 200mm. Most of these SLR lenses allow you to take images down to a 1:1 magnification. The biggest difference between film and digital SLR close-ups is the approximately 1.5 magnification factor that occurs with digital CCD SLR cameras.

Plus Diopters. You can also attain a variety of added close-up magnifications with SLR lenses by attaching a diopter lens. These close-up lens filters generally come in a set that range from +1 to +4 magnification (the higher the diopter number, the higher the magnification). The actual magnification factor will depend on the combination of the lens's focal length and the diopter of the close-up filter. There is also a special +10 diopter filter, referred to as a lifesizer, that allows you force the focus range of a normal lens down to a 1:1 magnification range.

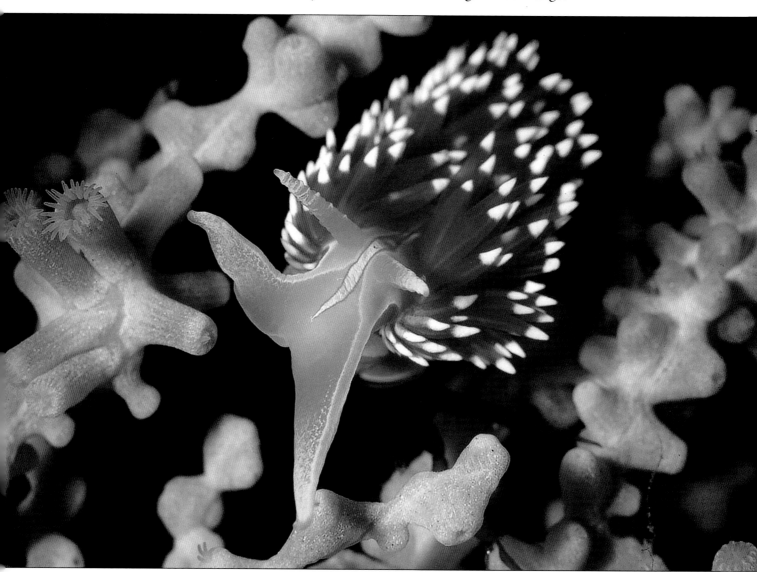

A macro lens set to 1:1 allowed us to get a very close view of this California nudibranch.

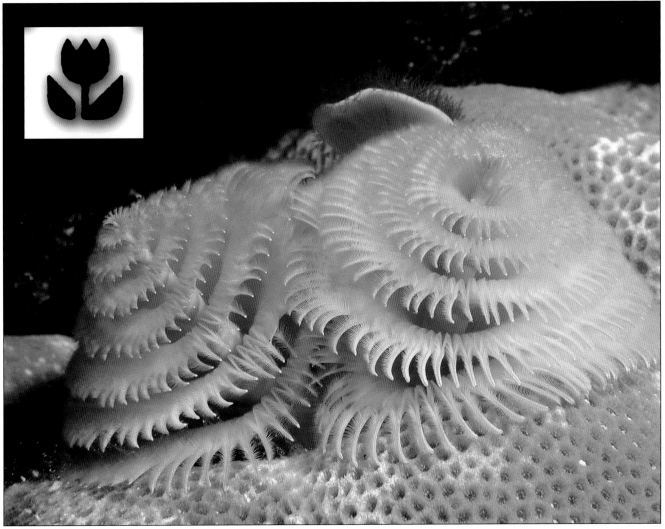

The flower icon on digital point & shoot cameras indicates that the camera's lens has been reconfigured so as to focus closely on small subjects.

Since the diopter will add some length to your SLR lens, you need to be sure that it still fits in your underwater housing. Extend the lens to its full expansion with the diopter attached and check that the combination does not bump into the lens port. If it does not fit, you will have to purchase a port extension tube to accommodate the added lens length.

Digital Point & Shoot Close-Ups. The digital point & shoot camera has brought us the most versatile close-up system to date. When the standard flower icon is pressed, the zoom elements inside the camera reconfigure themselves so that the camera can focus closer. A big advantage to this type of close-up camera is that you can frame and focus the subject on the back of the camera and get results similar to those once reserved for only the high-end SLR cameras.

Best of all, if you see a manta swimming off in the distance, you can turn off the flower icon, and the camera reconfigures the zoom lens for normal focusing distances. With this type of system, you will have the ability to capture just about every size of animal from a 40-ton whale down to a miniature nudibranch.

Of course not much in this world is perfect, so there is a downside to the close-up function on the point & shoot camera. When the flower icon is used, it takes longer for the camera to focus and shoot. If you have a fast-moving subject, it might well be gone before you fire off the shot. You will need to pick and choose your subjects when using this close-up function. If your subject is not too small, you might consider using the magnification properties of the zoom lens to achieve the close-up effect. When in the zoom mode, the camera

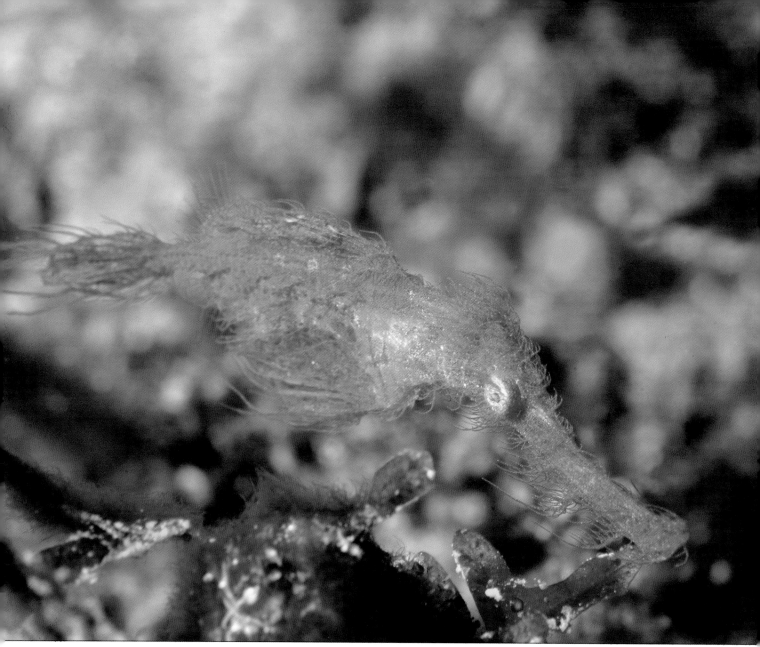

A digital SLR camera with a 105mm macro lens was used to photograph this very rare pipe fish. A twin-flash system was used to evenly light the subject.

fires more quickly than when in the flower close-up mode.

Single and Double Flash. When shooting magnifications of 1:10 down to 1:1, the best results come from using a twin-flash system in order to eliminate any harsh shadows. We have found the best combination is a larger flash unit as the main flash, set at a 45 degree angle to the subject. A second smaller flash should be set on the opposite side of the housing, close to the camera. It will serve to lightly fill in the dark shadows left by the main flash.

When you approach 1:1 magnification, you might find that a single flash will work fine if it is held in close to the camera lens. You may even be surprised to find that the built-in flash found in many of the digital point & shoot cameras will do a good job. The size of its flash tube is similar enough to the subject size that it will produce soft lighting. The problem is that it is a direct flash with no options for varying its direction. Therefore, the best option is still auxiliary flashes, so you can vary the flash angle and output.

High Speed Macro Flash. When you use an electronic flash underwater, much of the exposure control is with TTL, or automation within the flash. Essentially, once a correct exposure is achieved, the flash power is cut off before all power is dumped through the flash tube. When all the power is dumped, the flash duration is around $\frac{1}{1500}$ second. This fast speed will stop almost any movement. There will be times though, when the current is running and you are shooting very small critters, that this combination will cause a slight loss of sharpness even at the $\frac{1}{1500}$ second flash duration.

The solution is to increase the camera's ISO, move the flash closer, or open up the aperture so that less power is needed from the flash. When you do, the flash will fire at half power which will result in a $\frac{1}{3000}$ second flash duration. This increase in speed results in a sharper close-up image.

If you are still having problems, then modify the ISO, aperture, or flash distance again so that you are running at $\frac{1}{8}$ power. Your equivalent flash duration will be $\frac{1}{12000}$ second. If even that doesn't stop the action, then you might consider some software solutions, as noted on page 93.

■ DEPTH OF FIELD

One of the more difficult aspects of close-up photography is controlling depth of field. When the camera lens aperture is wide open, the only thing in focus is at the exact focus point itself. As the magnification factor increases, this extremely narrow focus point becomes even more reduced. The solution is to stop the lens aperture down. This reduces the amount of light coming through the lens, but it increases the range of focus on each side of the focus point, called the depth of field. This depth of field is at its maximum when the lens is stopped down to the smallest available aperture (the largest number).

Some of the very timid animals can only be captured using an SLR camera, very long macro lens, and a twin-flash system to soften the shadows.

FRAMER ENHANCERS

Many years ago, when we mainly took close-up images with a Nikonos and framers, we often found that there was a harsh shadow—even with twin lights. We researched the idea of using a reflector mounted to the underside of the framer and developed the Framer Enhancers. When a single flash was mounted above the camera lens, the light from the flash would light the subject from the top, then bounce off the reflector to light the subject from the bottom. This combination gave the effect of a strong main flash and a smaller fill flash. We eventually sold the invention to Aquatica (www .aquatic.ca). We find it still a great lighting solution when shooting with framers.

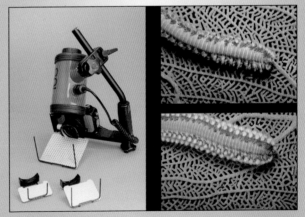

The Framer Enhancer attaches to the base of the film-camera framer and allows you to use a single flash and achieve reflected flash fill lighting. (The top photo is without the Framer Enhancer, the bottom one is with it.)

The problem is that most normal lenses start to lose their overall image sharpness as the lens is stopped down. Through years of testing lenses, we have found that most are sharpest when the camera lens is stopped down two to three stops from wide open. Macro lenses are the exception, as they are specifically designed to have their maximum sharpness at a stopped-down aperture. In addition, most of macro lenses have an extra one or two f/stops beyond the normal camera lens. It is not unheard of to find 50mm and 100mm macro lenses with a smallest aperture at f/32.

Digital Point & Shoot. For those jumping into a digital point & shoot camera after using a SLR macro lens, you might be concerned that its smallest aperture is only f/11. You might assume that the depth-of-field potential is much less than with the SLR—but not so! Consider the fact that most digital point & shoot camera chips are only a quarter the size of a 35mm film frame. Using the laws of photographic physics, you will see that, as the format becomes smaller, the f/stop needed to achieve the same depth of field is proportionally less. In most cases today, you can use two times the digital f/stop to get the equivalent f/stop in 35mm film. For example, the depth of field on an f/11 point & shoot digital would be the same as f/22 on an SLR camera.

Subject Angles. There will be some situations where, no matter how much you stop the lens down, you still cannot get the entire subject in focus. When in doubt, the solution is to focus on the subject's eyes and

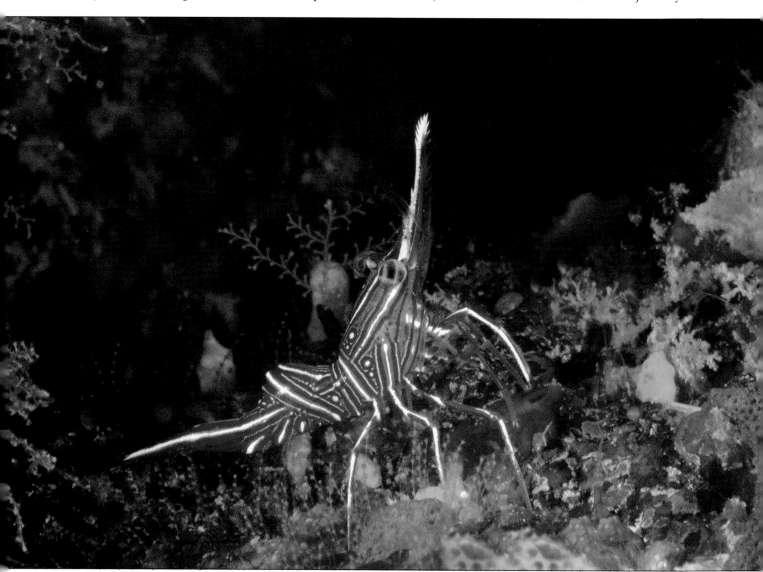

By keeping your camera parallel to the animal as you take its photo, you maximize your depth of field.

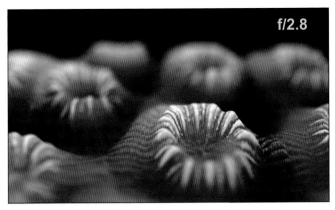

f/2.8

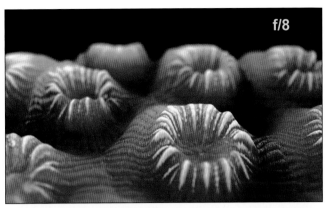

f/8

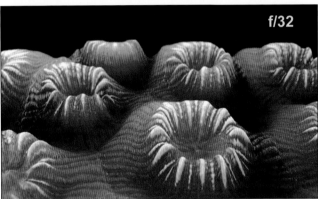

f/32

This series of images of hard coral shows the different depth-of-field effects created as you use smaller lens apertures.

let the rest slowly fade out of focus. Remember that one third of your total available depth of field falls *in front of* your focus point and two thirds falls *behind* it.

If you really need everything in focus, you will have to consider some additional camera angles to gain some added depth of field. Move your camera so that you are parallel to the subject rather than photographing it head on. This will produce the depth of field required to keep everything in focus.

■ SOFTWARE SOLUTIONS

When you looked at your macro images on the LCD finder underwater, they looked sharp. But when you take a second glance once back on the boat, you find some movement. Is there any hope of salvaging these images? At press time, there was a third-party plug-in filter for Adobe Photoshop called Focus Magic (www .focusmagic.com) designed to reverse both the effects of soft focus due to lens aberration or camera movement. This software is a must for those photographers demanding the highest sharpness standards in their underwater close-up images.

13. Super Macro

In recent years, innovative photographic technologies have made it possible for underwater photographers to expand their search into the world of super macro. Shooting images beyond 1:1 magnification has always been a very difficult task, yielding few rewards. Depth of field is almost nonexistent—often less than 1mm even when the lens aperture is stopped all the way down. Adding to the challenge is the need to deal with strong currents and low lighting levels.

So, why the interest in taking underwater images at such a small scale? The answer will be obvious the first time you take a magnified look at the reef and discover the treasures that most divers just swim past. You will find hundreds of strange new creatures with bizarre shapes and colors that, at times, look like they came from a science-fiction movie. It's a very exciting part of underwater photography and presents a challenge well worth exploring. We have spent more then 35 years in the quest for better super-macro images, and now present some samples in the hope that they will stimulate you to discover our world of the super macro.

■ WHAT IS SUPER MACRO?

Just so we are on the same page, our definition of super macro is images that have magnification factors greater than 1:1 and less than 10:1. See the previous chapter for more on close-up and macro definitions.

■ SHOOTING BEYOND 1:1

One of the earliest methods of shooting super-macro was with the Nikonos camera, extension tubes, and framers. Over the years, these tubes and framers became

This 2:1 magnification was taken with a Nikonos 5, 28mm lens, extension tubes, and a single flash using color slide film.

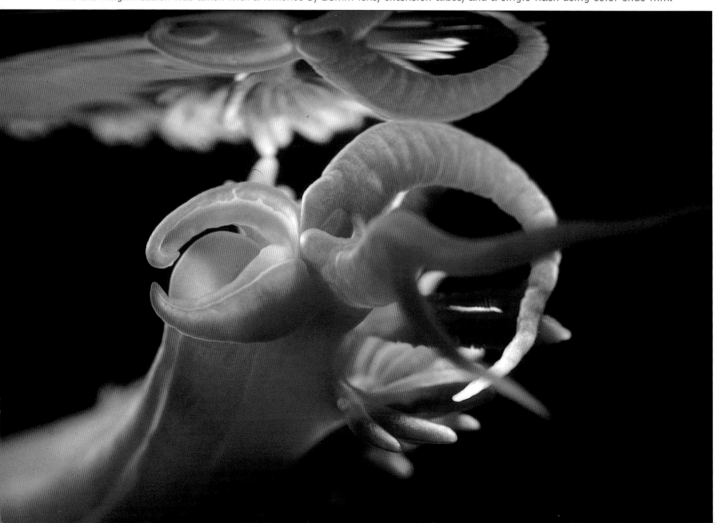

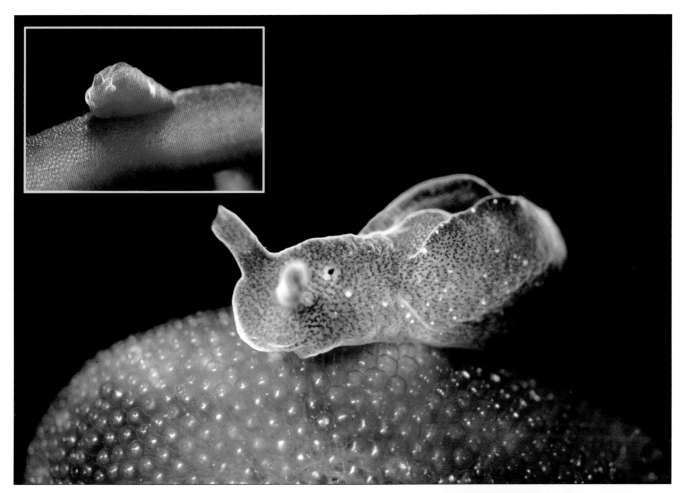

ABOVE—This 10:1 magnification of a nudibranch was taken with a special film housing fitted with a low powered microscope objective. These two images show the animal documented with both standard slide film and infrared slide film (inset).
RIGHT—A reflective Framer Enhancer has been added to this special super-macro setup with a Nikonos 5 and 2:1 framer.

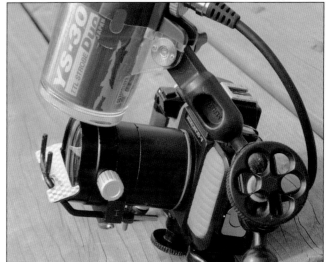

available for both the 35mm and 28mm lenses. Both had framers from 1:3 down to 1:1 magnification, but only the 35mm lens had a 2:1 super-macro framer that used a combination of two extension tubes. The problem was that this combination did not work very well, because the lens sharpness deteriorated and you rarely found any acceptable images on an entire roll of 36.

Our solution was to use the 28mm lens, as it was much sharper. We modified the 2:1 framer so that it was set to the correct focus distance. The 28mm still didn't work well, though, because the framer was too close to the lens for a flash to front-light the subject. To solve the problem, we decided to make one of our Framer Enhancers (see page 91) to fit the small 2:1 framer. This added reflected light to the base of the image when we placed a very small flash at the top of the framer. This allowed the flash to light the top portion of the image and then bounce some of its light onto the reflector to evenly light the bottom portion. We used this very compact system as our primary super macro system for years. If you are a film shooter and want to delve into the area of super macro, this is a great way to go.

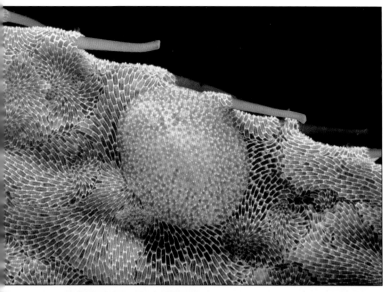

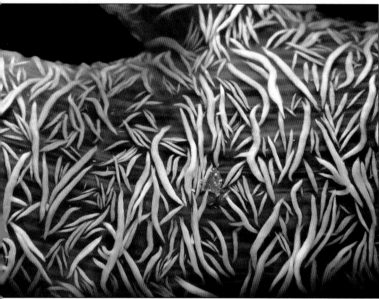

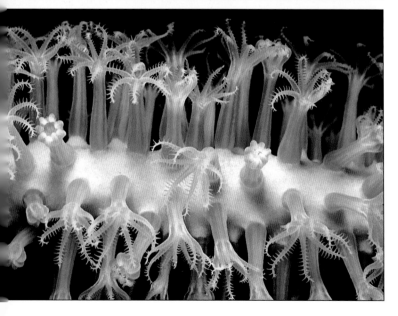

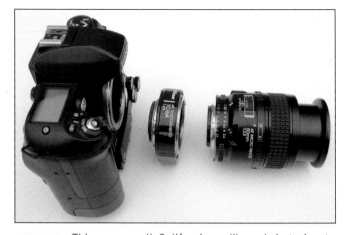

TOP LEFT—This very small California nudibranch is trying to camouflage and hide from the 2:1 Nikonos framer setup previously shown. MIDDLE LEFT—This Fijian soft coral demonstrates a 2:1 close-up using a digital SLR camera system and a tele-extender. BOTTOM LEFT—These soft coral polyps were taken with a digital SLR, 105mm macro lens, and a +4 diopter filter, which gave an effective magnification of 2:1. ABOVE—The digital SLR camera can extend its magnification range even further by adding tele-extenders.

■ TELE-EXTENDERS

This solution is great for both film and digital SLR shooters. Tele-extenders are like extension tubes, except that they have additional lens elements inside the tube. They are normally mounted between the camera body and a telephoto lens, so that the focal length of the lens can be magnified by factors from 1.5X to 2X. You can also use tele-extenders to increase your macro magnification up to two times. That may not seem like a lot of difference, but every bit of magnification in the super macro world appears enormous.

Digital SLR shooters with CCD chips have a big advantage over film shooters because they already have a 1.5 increase due to the magnification factor of CCD chips. If you add the tele-extender and the CCD chip's magnification together, you can have as high as a 3:1 magnification factor.

■ DIOPTERS

In most cases, you will need to add a macro port extension to your housing in order to accommodate the added length of the tele-extender. If you don't want the added expense of the macro extension port, you can add a +3 or +4 diopter to the front of the macro lens inside the housing, and extend your magnification up to

1.5X. Since most SLR camera ports have a small space in the front for other filters, you should be able to add this filter without making any changes to the housing. Carefully extend the lens to be sure that it doesn't exceed the space allocation. Keep in mind that when you add the diopter filter, you are restricted to high-magnification shooting during the entire dive and cannot shoot any lower magnifications until the filter is removed.

If you want more flexibility with the diopter filter and SLR housing, there are wet-lens diopters that fit over the front lens port. Using these filters alone, or in combination with a tele-extender inside the housing, can yield even greater magnification ratios.

■ POINT & SHOOT SUPER MACRO

We are starting to see a second close-up flower mode in some of the newer digital point & shoot models. It configures the zoom lens so it can shoot at magnifications beyond 1:1. In almost all cases, the lens is locked into one focal length, so if you want to shoot at other magnifications, you will have to reset the mode in the menu. This super-macro feature is great, because now you can use one camera to photograph wide-angles, general scenes, close-ups, *and* super macro—all on one dive!

■ WET-LENS SUPER MACRO

If you have an older digital point & shoot camera that does not support super-macro capabilities, don't

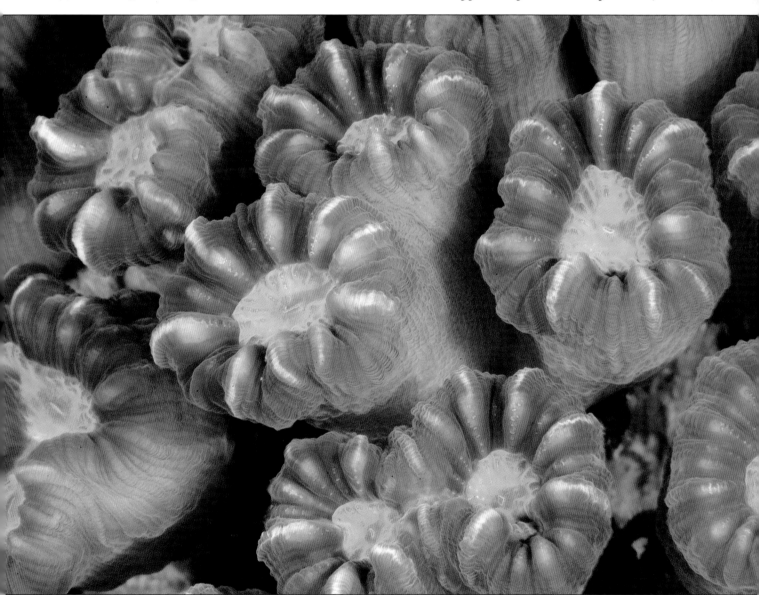

A 2:1 close-up of hard coral was taken with a point & shoot camera that had a super macro flower icon setting.

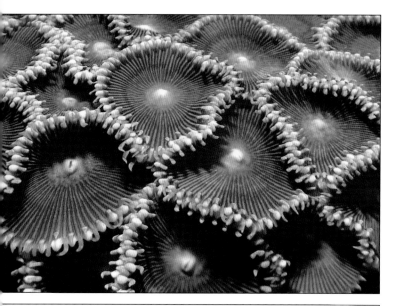

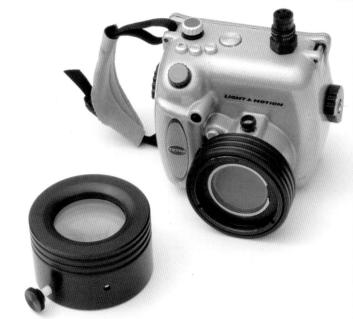

TOP—This intricate coral colony was captured with the super-macro wet lens attachment previously illustrated. BOTTOM—This is one of the super macro wet-lens attachments for point & shoot digital-camera housings.

correct exposure. Opening the aperture is not a viable solution, since your depth of field is already limited. The only solution is to use a higher ISO film. The two best slide film choices are Fuji Velvia 100 and Kodak Ektachrome 100. Using higher speed transparency films usually creates more grain, so the best option is to push the ISO 100 slide film one stop if necessary.

Color negative film users can choose either Fuji Superia or Kodak Supra in ISO 200 or 400 to get the best results. Although there will be some grain increase in the color negative images, it can be effectively reduced on a computer-editing system using Kodak Digital GEM Pro (www.asf.com). The combination of the higher speed color negative film and this innovative plug-in will allow you to create some very impressive super macro images.

Digital camera users don't have to worry about grain, but rather digital camera noise. The increase to ISO 400 or even 800 to get acceptable exposures with your super macro will only show a little image quality loss. Even then, there is a third party plug-in filter for Adobe Photoshop called Dfine (www.nikMultimedia .com). It reduces the digital camera noise to a point where it is nonexistent, while still keeping the images very sharp.

despair. You might consider one of the new close-up lens adapters that take your point & shoot camera to almost 2:1 magnification. The best part of these lenses is that they can be removed underwater, so you can continue using all the other focus modes that the camera supports.

ISO CONSIDERATIONS

Super-macro photography requires very small f/stops and extreme subject magnification, so it takes a large amount of light on the subject to get a decent exposure. Film users may find that their combination of camera, lens, and flash will not produce enough light to get a

ADDING AUXILIARY LIGHTS

When working with any of the super-macro systems we have mentioned, you will find that the light falling on the subject is generally far too low to enable accurate viewing for framing and focus. This applies to both film and digital users. It is very important that you add some type of wide-beam flashlight to your system to make it easier to clearly see what you are shooting. In most cases, the light will need to be mounted one top of the housing and manually aimed. Make sure that it doesn't have a concentrated light beam; otherwise it will create a hotspot in the image. If the flashlight has too much of a focused beam, you may have to put a diffuser on it to provide even lighting.

■ FACE-MASK CONFIGURATIONS

In your quest for tiny subjects, you may find that you have difficulty clearly seeing what you are trying to photograph, even if you don't normally need glasses. The solution is to put a small diopter in your face mask that allows you to see higher magnifications. Not only will this help you better see the small subjects, but it also enables you to see the housing controls and text on the LCD menu screen.

If your mask has separate left and right eyepieces, another solution would be to get a full diopter for one side that allows you to see a few inches away from your mask and leave the other side without any correction. The first dive might be a little disconcerting, but the human brain has the ability to adjust to such a visual configuration. In time, you will be able to see clearly from a few inches to infinity.

We have also seen a few divers who use a plastic hand-held magnifying glass. It is a handy and inexpensive way to see camera menus and animals alike.

■ SOFTWARE MAGNIFICATION

When you have done your best to magnify the image as much as possible during the photographic process but still find the subject too small in the image, there is still hope. You might consider using Adobe Photoshop to

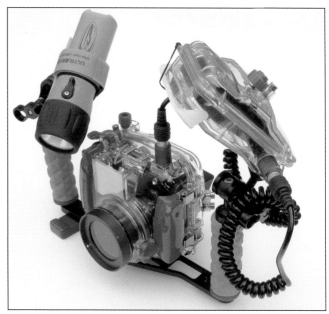

When shooting macro images, a wide-beam flashlight is handy to help with focusing and framing, even in bright sunlight.

first enlarge the entire image, and then crop it to produce a higher magnification. Another option is computer software designed to enlarge, sharpen, and scale the image to a much larger image magnification. The best two of these programs are third party Adobe Photoshop plug-ins called Genuine Fractals Print Pro from www.lizardtech.com and SmartScale, available from www.extensis.com.

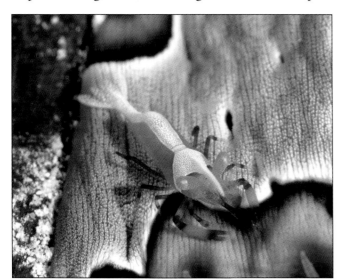
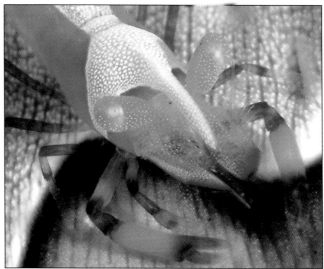

The image on the left shows how you can take images at 1:1 magnification with your digital camera and then further increase the magnification using editing software (right).

14. Backscatter

Backscatter is one of the most difficult aspects of underwater photography to overcome and it is totally unique to the underwater realm. It exists everywhere underwater, so your method for handling it will make the difference between producing a so-so photo and a professional-looking underwater image.

◼ ANATOMY OF A BACKSCATTER PARTICLE

Backscatter is nothing more than small sediment, plants, and small creatures floating in the water. When these particles are illuminated, the contrast of the light striking the particles against the dark background forms bright highlights that resemble falling snow.

These particles are the least visible in available light, because the light falling on the particles and the background is equal. On the other hand, when you light a scene using electronic flash it is much stronger than the available light, which highlights the particles. Underwater photography at night is the worst-case scenario, because the range between the flash on the particles in relationship to the black background is the most extreme.

In order to fully understand how to control backscatter in your images, you first must understand the various photographic situations that present this

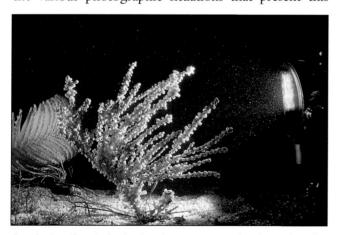

By placing the strobe in the photo, you can clearly see how its beam highlights backscatter particles.

high range of contrast in lighting. In each of the situations, we will show you the cause for backscatter and then offer a solution for that specific problem. From there, you can work on changing your photo techniques in order to minimize the backscatter. Keep in mind that you can't *totally* get rid of backscatter; the best you can hope for is to *hide* it.

◼ CAUSES OF BACKSCATTER

Flash Too Close to the Camera. One of the most common causes of backscatter is the placement of the flash too close to the camera lens. Since the lighting contrast is very strong in front of the flash, it will light all the particles that are floating between the camera lens and the subject. This is a common problem with the smaller film or digital point & shoot cameras that have a built-in flash. These flashes are usually positioned right over the lens, and they concentrate their light directly towards the particles in front of the camera lens.

One solution is to diffuse the flash, which will in effect reduce the harsh lighting. Most of the newer point & shoot housings on the market have some kind of diffuser system to help spread the light over a larger area. Even when diffused, though, these internal flashes tend to light the backscatter, so use them sparingly.

A better solution is to completely block the internal flash and reflect its light upwards or to the side so that it can trigger a slave flash. The auxiliary flash can then be moved away from the camera lens to minimize the backscatter. Even some of the older flash units, like the Nikonos 105, feature a built-in slave function.

Another method is to use a fiber-optic cable to trigger an auxiliary flash like those found on the Sea & Sea MX-10 (film) and DX-3000 (digital) point & shoot camera systems. With these cameras, a special sync port is found on both the camera housing and Sea & Sea compatible flash. It connects the light path from the camera's internal flash to the external flash via a fiber-

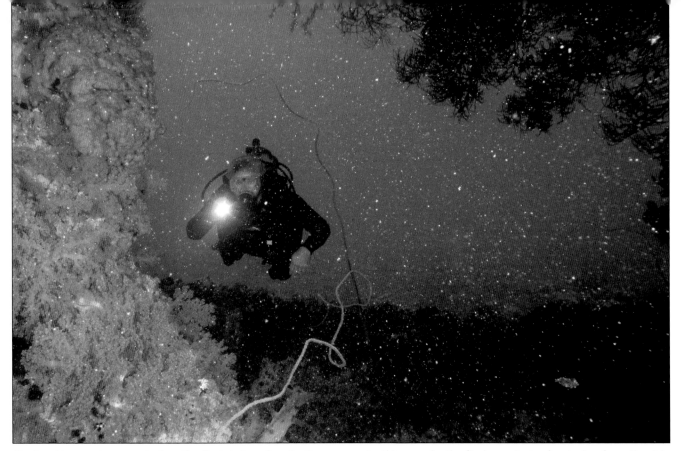

Backscatter can be caused when the flash is too close to the camera. In this sample, the flash was just a few inches from the side of the camera.

optic cable. When the camera is fired, the light flows from the flash through the cable to a sensor on the flash. For systems without these ports, there are Velcro kits that attach ports to both the camera housing and flash, so almost any point & shoot camera system can be outfitted with fiber optic sync capability.

Point & shoot film cameras are pretty reliable when using these types of slave flash-sync systems, but digital is a bit more difficult. Many of the digital point & shoot cameras have pre-flash functions that focus, white balance, and check exposure before firing the main flash. Any of these pre-flash firings may set off the external flash prematurely. For this reason, a new type of digital flash has been designed which bypasses the pre-flash and fires in sync with the main flash. Some units, like the Sea & Sea DX-25, have multiple pre-flash settings to better match up with the multitude of digital point & shoot cameras on the market.

As the digital world flexes its muscles, we expect to see even more underwater digital flash systems available. For example, Ikelite now has several digital auto flash sensors that attach to Ikelite camera housings. They act as flash negotiators between a wide variety of digital cameras and Ikelite strobes. Thankfully, manufacturers continue to design new innovations to help make underwater photography easier.

One of the best ways to get distance between your flash and camera housing is by means of a hard-wired sync cord. Almost all SLR housings today use this type of sync-cord connection, which allows you the flexibility to move your flash to any position in an effort to avoid backscatter. Again, digital housings have an advantage, as you can take a test shot, check the results in the LCD viewfinder, and then move the flash to a better position and try it again.

We are now starting to see hot shoes on some of the higher-resolution point & shoot digital cameras. As housing manufacturers start incorporating external ports and hot-shoe sync cords, the point & shoot photographer will soon have the same advantages as the digital SLR user.

Subject Too Far From the Camera Lens. Another cause of backscatter is when there is considerable distance from the camera lens to the subject. This generally happens when you use a normal or short-telephoto lens underwater. It is a simple fact that the greater the water column between the the lens and the subject, the more particles there are to light with the flash.

The first solution is to use a wider-angle lens, which reduces the water column and puts you closer to the subject. This is why most professional underwater photographers have an arsenal of wide and super-wide lenses that they take on dive trips. With wide-angle lenses, you can be inches away from a very large subject, keep everything in focus, and only light a few particles.

If your camera and lens configuration requires that you use a longer focal-length lens, as when photographing fish, you can remove the flash diffuser and move the flash out and away from the camera lens. This will cause the flash's narrow beam of light to project only on the

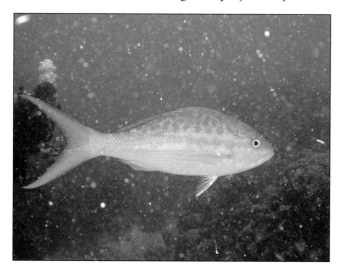

subject, without lighting any particles between the lens and the subject.

Lighting Contrast. As the light levels drop, the lighting ratio from the flash-lit foreground to the sun-lit background starts to increase. This causes the illuminated backscatter particles to become more distinct against the dark background. This problem occurs mainly during early morning, late afternoon, or on night dives.

One of the first things you can do is to add a second flash, so that the backscatter particles are evenly illuminated on both sides. Then you can adjust the ratio of flash to sun-lit background so that both are have the same intensity. With most auto and TTL systems, this is a very difficult task. Your best option is to go to the manual exposure mode. Then, you can reduce the shutter speed to increase the background exposure and adjust the flash output to match the available-light exposure.

Over the years, film users have had to depend on light meters, guide numbers, and extensive pre-testing

LEFT—When the distance from the front of the lens to the subject increases, particles lit by the flash become more obvious. BELOW—This self portrait with a very large, friendly octopus was shot by holding a Nikonos and 15mm lens at arm's length. The short focus distance reduced the water column and backscatter particles.

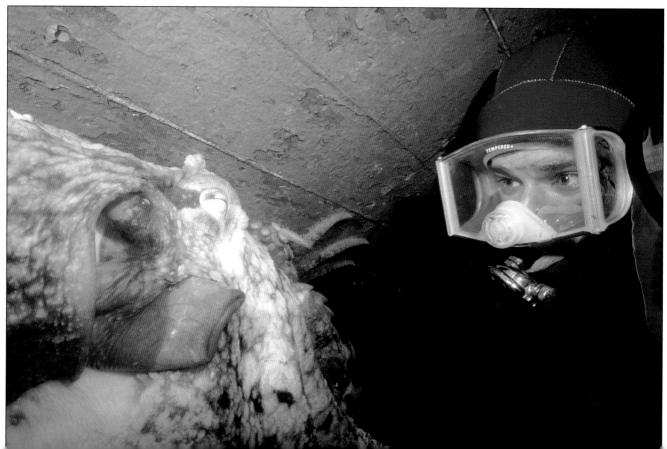

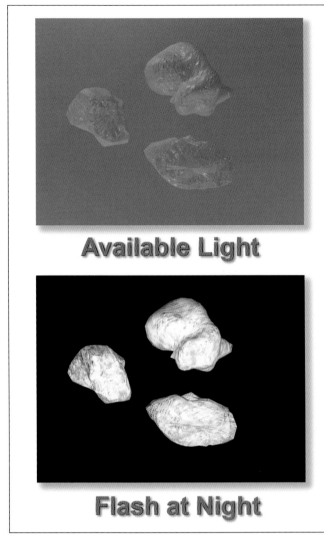

Available Light

Flash at Night

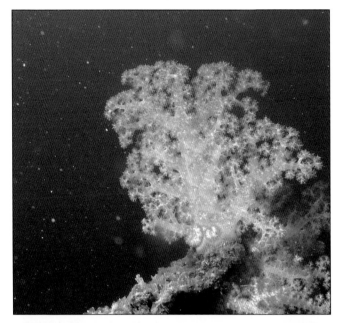

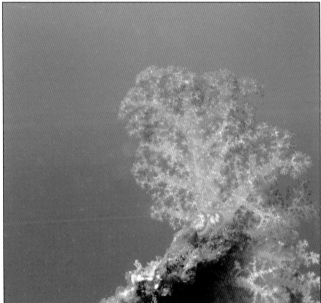

ABOVE—As the lighting contrast between the background and the backscatter particles increases, the particles become more obvious to the viewer. RIGHT—These two photos demonstrate how backscatter particles become more obvious as the background exposure darkens.

to ensure a good blend between foreground and background exposures. With digital, it is much easier. All you have to do is shoot, review, adjust, and reshoot until you have a good balance (see chapter 7 on exposure). Digital point & shoot cameras have the most control over backscatter since you can use the entire range of shutter speeds and aperture settings to get the balance. The digital SLR cameras are still restricted to the flash-sync speed when setting the shutter speed, so often it is harder to achieve a good balance. If, during the adjustment process, you find that the shutter speed is too low or the lens aperture too wide, you also have the option with digital to modify the ISO setting from image to image. Each time you change the ISO on your digital camera, check the viewer until you have a balance that works.

Obviously this solution will not work on night dives since there is no sunlight. In this situation, your first choice is to move the flash as far from the camera as possible to reduce the backscatter. The dirtier the water, the farther away the flash must be from the camera lens. Another easy solution for night dives is to top-, side-, or backlight the subject so that none of the particles have direct front lighting. This is a great technique for fire coral and other subjects with fine, transparent detail along the edge of the animal.

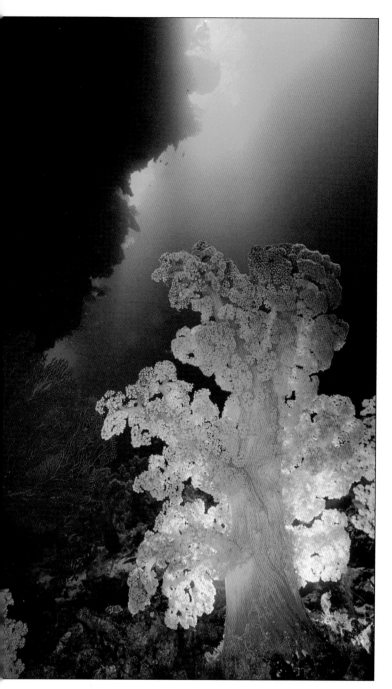

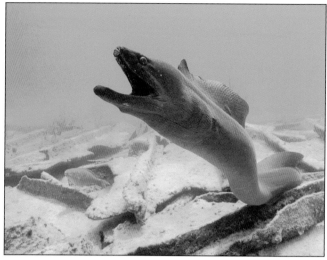

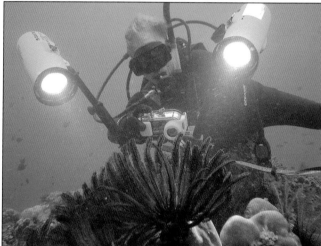

LEFT—One method for reducing backscatter is to place the flash behind the subject. TOP RIGHT—This shallow dive had heavy backscatter. The solution was to turn the flash off and use the lower-contrast available light as the main light source. BOTTOM RIGHT—This wreck in the Solomons had very dirty water, so we used the tungsten lights of another diver to light the scene.

■ EXTREME BACKSCATTER

There will be situations when the water visibility is very low due to a heavy concentration of dirt particles. This is common when in heavy currents, shallow water, near shipwrecks, or if you encounter extreme changes in water temperature. In many of these situations, none of the previously mentioned solutions will effectively reduce the backscatter. Not to worry, though—we have more stuff in our bag of tricks.

The easiest solution when you encounter heavy backscatter is simply to turn off the flash. Since both the background and foreground lighting is very soft, the backscatter will only show minimally.

If you still want a spot of color in the image, you can have a diver in the distance turn on a flashlight and point it toward you. This flashlight, when used in area with heavy backscatter, will produce a light beam just like in the Hollywood movies. This is also a very effective tool when shooting in caves or on shipwrecks. The same effect can also be created by using a small on-camera flash pointed away from the scene to trigger a distant flash held by another diver.

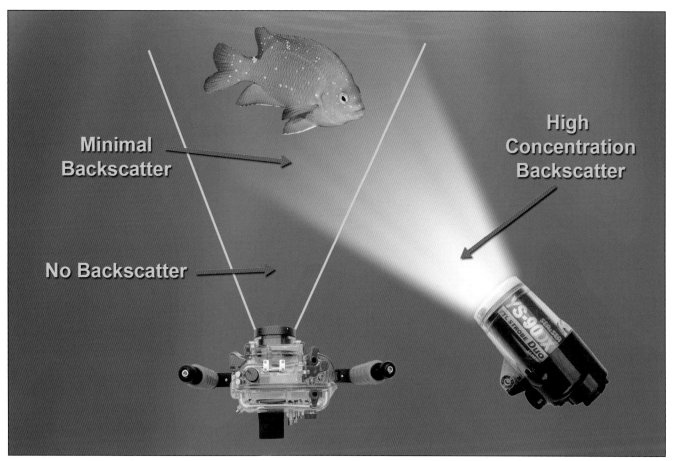

This illustration shows a typical flash setup if there is only moderate backscatter in the water.

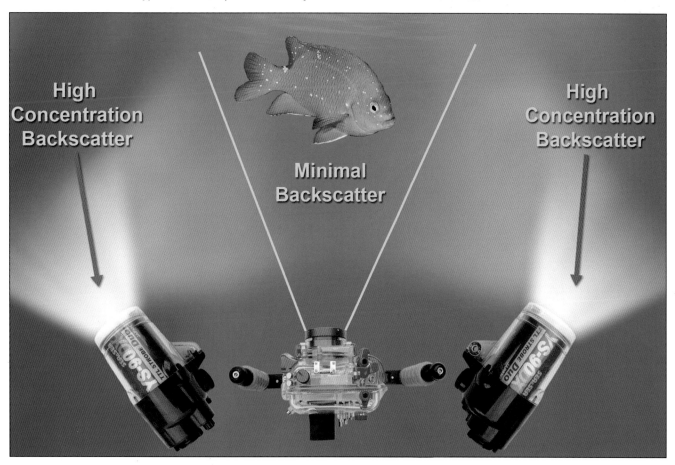

This illustration shows the flash position you need to use when you have extreme backscatter. You will have to use very wide apertures since most of the flash output is lost.

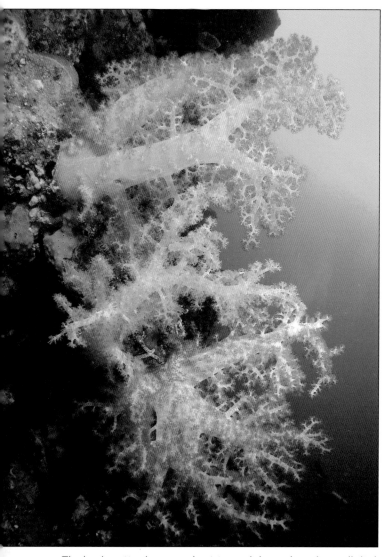

The backscatter here was kept to a minimum by using a digital SLR camera, super wide lens, and twin flashes on very long Ultralight arms.

You may find yourself in a situation where the particles are evident, but you still must use a flash. You can bounce the flash off the particles to create an underwater soft box effect just like the commercial studio photographers. This is done by pointing either one or two flash units (two works the best) at 45-degree angles away from the camera lens. This way, only the light bouncing off the particles will light the scene, producing a much softer lighting. The problem is that the light loss using this method is enormous. To compensate, you will have to use a large flash output, increase your ISO speed, and open the lens aperture to compensate—otherwise you will have an underexposure.

◼ WHEN ALL ELSE FAILS

There will be times when you find a rare creature that you are going to photograph no matter whether you get backscatter or not. You make every attempt using all the anti-backscatter solutions, but without success. Do you just swim past in hopes of seeing it again? No way. You can now use your ace in the hole: the computer. Go ahead and capture the critter as best as possible, using all your backscatter-removal resources. Then bring the image into your editing system, and you might be surprised at all of your editing options. Adobe Photoshop provides a wide variety of editing tools to help remove the backscatter. In fact, we have dedicated an entire chapter on backscatter removal in our book *Digital Imaging for the Underwater Photographer*, also from Amherst Media.

Great underwater photographs are a careful blend of both art and science. The science mainly involves the use of new digital technology to get the image correctly exposed, focused, and framed. The art is the action that happens behind the camera viewfinder or LCD viewer. The human eye and how it perceives an underwater scene can make the difference between a ho-hum image and one that jumps out and grabs you.

When most new underwater photographers start taking pictures, they feel lucky if they have accomplished the scientific part and were able to document the scene or animal. This first stage of underwater photography we call "taking" a picture. When photographers become more accomplished, they start to apply some creative approaches to their images and begin "making" underwater images. This means going beyond simply documenting the animal, but rather trying different angles, perspectives, and lighting to create more dramatic images.

Often, the key element that separates the *good* from the *great* photographer is the application of composition. It's this added visual impact that makes a viewer admire one photograph over another. Good composition is the result of structured guidelines and their artistic interpretation, which differs among photographers. If you are familiar with these rules and techniques from your topside photography, you already have a head start on getting some great underwater images.

■ POSITIVE COMPOSITION

The interesting aspect of composition is that there are no rules set in stone, only guidelines. You can be assured that if you set a rule, someone will only break it with an outstanding image. The following compositional concepts should only be viewed as guidelines—a method of helping you build your own shooting style. We will first look at those compositional concepts that

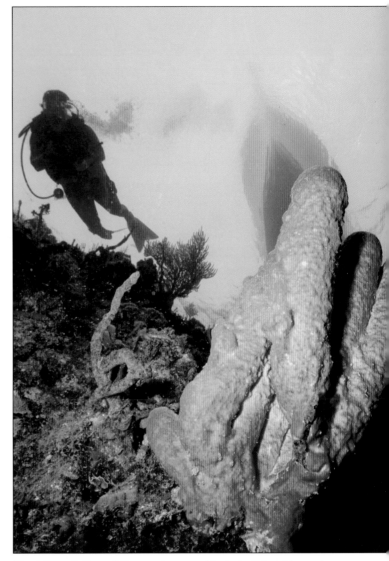

The triangulation of three primary subjects in this wide-angle image illustrates good composition.

provide a positive feel to an image, and later address those that tend to work against the photographer.

Rule of Thirds. When a single subject is photographed against a background, there is a tendency to place it in the center, but it is best placed in the ⅓ position in the frame. This position is determined by evenly spacing two vertical lines and two horizontal lines in the frame, dividing the image into nine distinct sec-

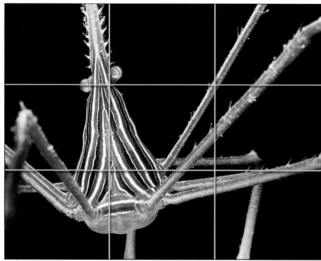

The eyes of this arrow crab are positioned at the intersection of two lines to create this ⅓ composition.

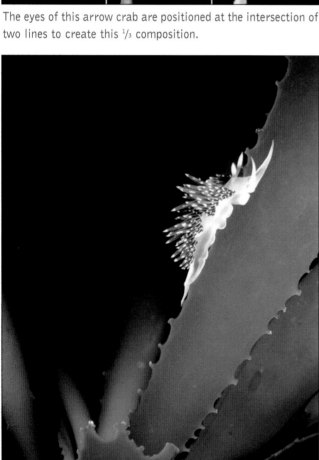

tions. Any of the points at which these lines intersect are subject positions that viewers find most pleasing to the eye. Many of the new digital cameras today have a built-in grid that simulates the ⅓ composition, which helps you to place the subject at one of the intersections. This grid is only visible in the LCD viewer and does not appear in your final image.

Lines Leading to a Point. Another dramatic form of composition is when a line enters the photograph from one side and flows through the image. For exam-

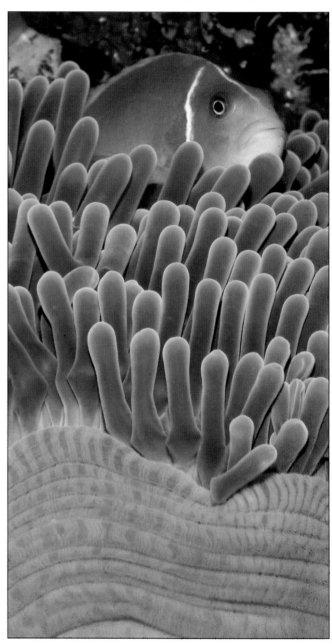

LEFT—This image of a nudibranch crawling up a kelp leaf uses diagonal lines that lead your eye to the subject in the ⅓ position. The result is a strong composition. RIGHT—The three layers of colors in this vertical format use color and shape to create a strong compositional form.

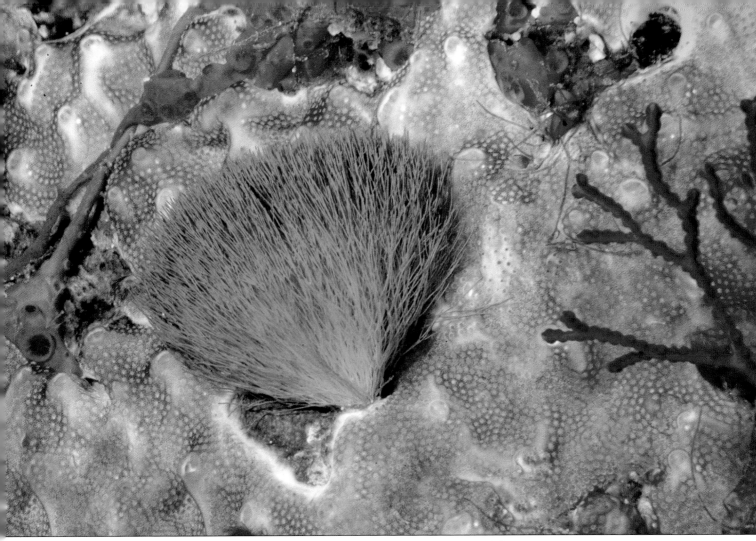

When you find two opposing colors, this contrast can create a very strong compositional form.

ple, imagine a sea fan, soft coral, or sea whip entering one side of the image and continuing to flow across the image to the other side of the frame. The most dramatic form of line composition is when there is a subject at the end of the line. For example, the center of a sea fan might lead your eye up to find a crinoid on the edge of the fan.

Color. The colors of the underwater world can be a very powerful compositional tool. A subject of one color on an opposite colored background can create a very dramatic image, especially if it is framed in the $\frac{1}{3}$ position.

You will find that contrasts between cool colors (like the blue or green background in available light) and warm colors (from the flash's illumination) are also used by wide-angle photographers to produce a dramatic composition.

Another composition trick is to find colored animals at rest on the same color background. This image draws the viewer's interest as it becomes a game of hide and seek, challenging the viewer to search for the red nudibranch on the red sponge.

Highlighting just a spot of color is a technique used to draw the viewer's eye into the main scene. A narrow beam flash can be used to light just the colored subject against a very large available-light background. The viewer's eye will tend to look at the overall image and then be quickly drawn to the small colorful subject. Again, placement of this object in a $\frac{1}{3}$ position will help reinforce the impact of the image.

Negative Space. This concept is popular with wide-angle photographers as it helps demonstrate the vastness of an underwater scene. In most cases, the diver or animal is placed in the lower portion of the image with a large open-water space above. This is best accomplished with a super wide-angle lens that allows you to get close to the subject yet, because of perspective distortion, still makes the subject appear small in the image. The lack of subject matter in the upper area of the image becomes a negative space. This is also the case where the subject doesn't necessarily need to have color to create a dramatic image. In fact, some of the

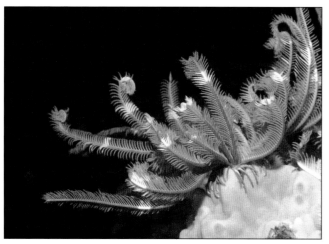

The negative space in the upper left adds balance to the image.

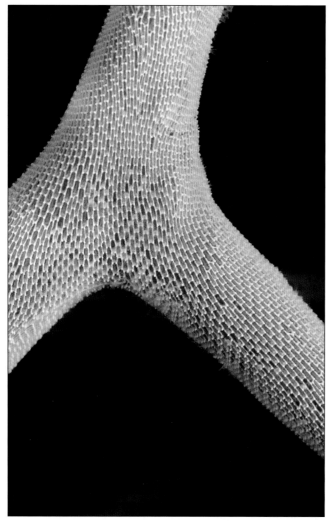

Bryozoan on a kelp frond forms a very simple upside-down Y composition.

more dramatic images have a black silhouette of the subject against the large negative background.

Letter Composition. Letter composition is a very popular type of topside photographic composition, but it also lends itself well to underwater photography. When looking at an underwater image, the human eye will perceive portions of the scene that form letter shape with more interest than those without. There are no rules as to which letter composition works the best, but some of the most popular are L, O, X, T, S, J, M, U, V, W, Y, and Z.

When you start looking for letter shapes in the sea, you may only find a few. You'll be surprised to find that the more you keep looking, the more you will discover. An easy one to find is an upside down U formed by the top and two sides of a cave. Another would be a sponge forming the O composition, a W might be a pattern in hard coral, and the Y might be the intersection of the veins in a sea fan.

Opposites Attract. Any image will have increased viewing interest whenever you have two subjects (or a subject and a background) that have opposite attributes. That can be almost anything: opposite colors, sharp and out of focus, low contrast and high contrast, high color saturation and low, large and small subjects, horizontal and vertical, and more. The key is to first recognizing the opposites, and then position your camera and frame the subjects so they best oppose each other. It causes the viewer's eye to move from one subject to the other and then back again. This type of image holds interest for a long time and can be a very powerful composition.

Point of View. Often, changing your point of viewing can dramatically alter the visual impact of an image. When marine biologists document animal life, their main goal is to obtain the best possible identification image. The underwater photographer needs to think beyond documentation and apply creativity by changing the angle, lighting, or perspective. This angle change is just a matter of moving to a different position, high or low, or by moving in closer to photograph only part of the animal. Just modify the lighting by moving the flash to a top-, side-, or backlight position. You might even adjust your shooting angle so that the sun lights the background.

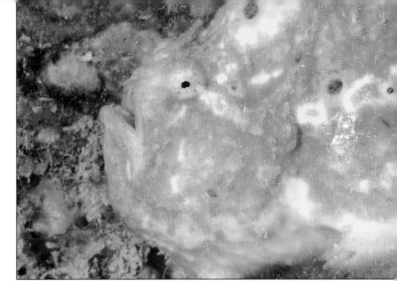

When you find a great subject, make sure that you try both vertical and horizontal images. You might be surprised which composition is the strongest.

Perspective changes are usually accomplished by using different wide-angle setups, as discussed in chapter 10. With these lenses, you can move in very close to a tiny subject and make it appear larger than the subject in the background. A perspective image of a tiny tube-worm appearing to be the same size as a diver can be very dramatic.

Patterns and Shapes. Up to now, we have talked about underwater scenes with a subject and background, but that doesn't always have to be the case for good composition. There are thousands of unique patterns and shapes found in the underwater world. Take a close-up look at coral, a sponge, or the surfaces of starfish and you'll find that the pattern or shape itself becomes the subject. This composition becomes even stronger if there are slight color changes in the image, minor variations within the pattern, or if it contains a small animal as an added point of interest. Keep in mind that those patterns that run diagonally in an image seem to have a stronger impact.

Framing. A key ingredient in good composition is proper framing. In order to have your main subject as the center of interest, it is best framed by other portions of the image that are specifically positioned to draw your eye to the main subject. Generally, this frame works best if it is dark in color, so as to create the proper eye flow toward the subject.

Cropping. For years, the film user composed an underwater image to be the final image output. Time and care had to be taken to make sure all the key image elements were contained in the 35mm film frame. Today, almost all images, both digital and film, pass through a computer-editing system before the final image is presented. This means that you have the option of cropping after the fact. You should still strive to edit within the camera, but if you find another cropping option looks better on the computer screen, don't be afraid to make that change.

■ NEGATIVE COMPOSITION

Up to now we have concentrated our discussion on the positive forms of composition—things that tend to

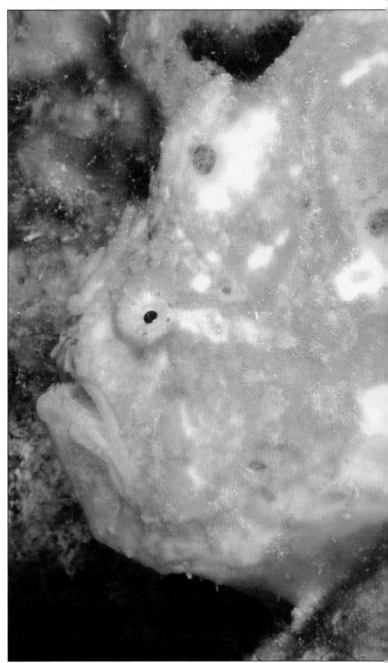

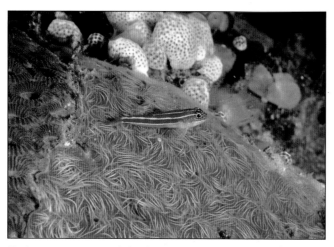
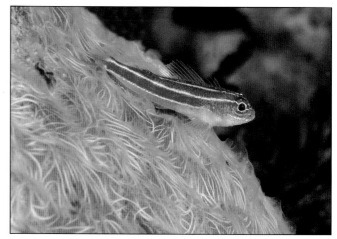

Trying to get too much in the image is a common mistake with new digital photographers. Move in, zoom your lens, change your angle, or crop the image later in your editing program.

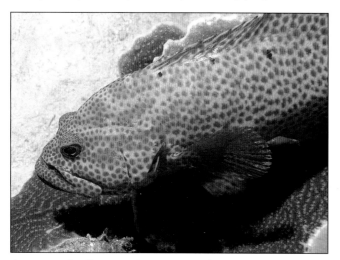
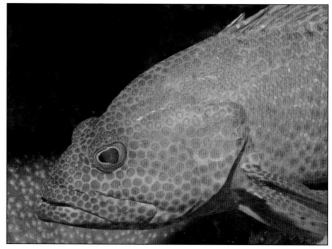

Just a small adjustment in camera angle can change the entire feel of the photo and eliminate the unsightly light trap.

make images look good. To really understand composition, though, you also need to see what creates *poor* composition or tends to diminish the overall creative impact of the image.

Busy Scenes. This is a common problem with new underwater photographers, as they get very excited about everything they see and want to include it *all* in their images. These busy images often have multiple subjects, all vying to capture the viewer's interest. The solution is to narrow your scope and selectively move in to capture just one or two subjects. You can also use a wider aperture to zero the focus on the subject and have the focus fade to the background.

Subject Too Close to the Edge. In the excitement of photographing animals, underwater photographers often don't pay enough attention to the area surrounding the subject. This results in the subject literally bumping into the edge of the image or scooting halfway out of the scene. It is best to shoot the subject with some area around it, then crop it later in the computer if necessary. When framing close to a subject like a fish, make sure you have space in front of the subject, so that it appears to have somewhere to swim. It is better to place more space in front of your subject than behind it.

Light Traps. Light traps are areas in the image that are much brighter than the subject itself. Since the human eye is drawn to the lightest area of the image, the subject is often lost. In most cases, these light areas are dead corals or subjects close to the edge of the frame that were highlighted by the flash.

You need to watch for light traps while shooting and reframe your image so that the light area does not appear in the final image. If the light trap is not possible to remove, you can later crop the image in the computer or selectively reduce the bright area with tools in your editing software.

Lacking Contrast, Color, or Sharpness. Before digital, most underwater images were taken on slide film, so what you photographed underwater was the final product. This resulted in images that were often lacking in color, contrast, and occasionally even sharpness. This was generally due to using the standard lens that came with the camera rather than the more expensive wide-angle lenses. A very high percentage of images ended up in the trash—images that could have been salvaged with today's computer software programs.

The best solution here is, first, to use the best equipment possible to capture the underwater world, whether with digital or film. Get as close to your subject as possible. Then, if necessary, you can adjust any image shortcomings using your image-editing software.

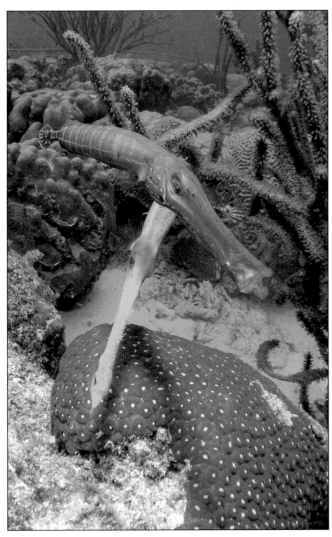

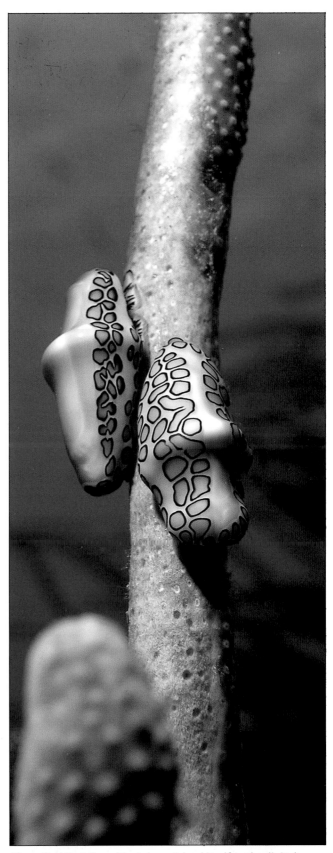

If you find that the subject doesn't lend itself to the digital camera format, shoot it anyway, and crop it later in your editing program.

16. Reef Protection and Photographic Ethics

When we first started our underwater photographic careers in 1970, the priorities for underwater photography were quite different than today. There was little worry for diver safety and almost no concern for reef protection. Today, new divers are being taught that diver safety comes first, the reef the second priority, and then comes photography.

Unfortunately, over the years, some underwater photographers have bashed into the reef while searching for that perfect photo. Their antics have placed a nasty label on all underwater photographers and it needs to be our goal to make things right. Underwater photographers have to be on their best reef-protection behavior and set a good example for new divers. There is no photograph so valuable that it warrants intentional reef or animal damage.

That said, we still want to take underwater photos, so we need to learn the necessary skills to do it safely. Here are a few tips on safely getting the photo yet still protecting the underwater world so it will be there for future generations to enjoy.

■ BUOYANCY SKILLS

Good buoyancy is the key to becoming a good underwater photographer. It should be a skill that all divers master before ever attempting to take a camera underwater. You should be comfortable in your surroundings and you should be able to raise or lower yourself along

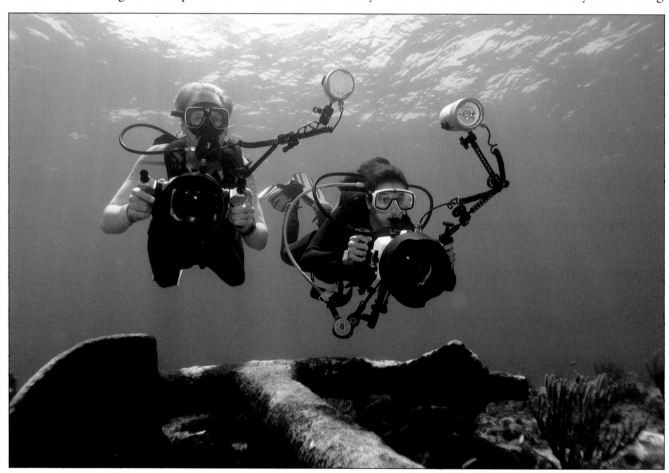

Digital photographers today must be very good with buoyancy, so that they do not damage the reef.

the reef merely by using breath control. You shouldn't need to constantly kick your fins to hold your position. Remember that the more you use your fins, the greater the potential you will add to the backscatter by stirring up sediment near the bottom.

One of the best ways to hone your buoyancy skills is to take your camera system down and try to approach a rock formation by getting within a few inches of it without actually touching it. Remember that each change to your camera, housing or flash configuration, may factor in the weight necessary to achieve good buoyancy. Once you have a good feeling for buoyancy control, you are ready to move onto this next step.

■ THE DEAD ZONE

Over the years, aggressive steps have been taken to protect the reefs. We now see no-touch, no-gloves, and no-animal-feeding rules. Many of these concepts are great, but unfortunately each dive resort uses different rules, so there is no constant that divers can go by. The no-touch system works fine in calm water areas, but it's a disaster if you are in currents or surge. New divers are told they cannot touch the reef under any circumstances, and more often than not, they end up crashing on the reef because a small surge hit them from behind.

We have studied the problem for years and offer a solution that features reef protection, but can be accomplished by divers of all skill levels. We call it "Staying in Touch with the Dead Zone" and here's how it works. As you swim along the reef and spot an animal that deserves a closer inspection or a photograph, take a minute to first check your surroundings. Scan the reef for rocks or coral near the animal that have dead areas. Unfortunately, that has become easier to do with the slow death of the world's coral reefs today.

Slowly approach the animal and place a single finger in this dead zone to hold yourself off the reef before ever attempting to take a picture. If the current is coming towards you, you can use your fins to help maintain constant pressure between your finger and the dead zone. This single point of contact on the reef provides you an enormous amount of control and stability, even in heavy surge. Once you have insured that you are indeed stable, you can safely take your shot, knowing that you will not damage the reef.

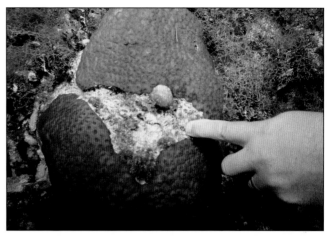

Use one finger in a dead zone to keep yourself off the reef when taking pictures.

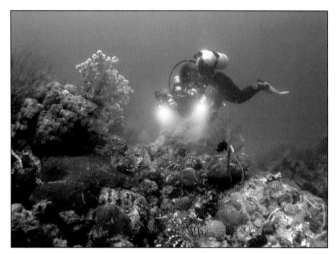

This underwater photographer can safely hold herself off the reef while she photographs the animals by demonstrating good buoyancy and a single-finger hold in a dead zone.

■ TIME OUTS

No matter how skilled a diver you are, there will come a time when you accidentally bump into a part of the reef and damage occurs. When this happens, you need to immediately stop what you are doing, and back off the reef. Take a time out, and analyze why it happened, and how you can prevent any future accidents. You should never consider a photograph more important than the reef. If you continue to find yourself having problems, you might consider a refresher buoyancy class to update and improve your diving skills.

■ PHOTOGRAPHIC ETHICS

There was a time, not too long ago, when underwater photographers moved animals from one location to another to get a better shot. There were those who mis-

INTERACTING WITH ANIMALS

There are some locations that endorse man–animal inter-action. For example, Stingray City in the Cayman Islands is a popular dive spot controlled by Cayman authorities who have determined that divers interacting with the animals is acceptable and will not damage the reef.

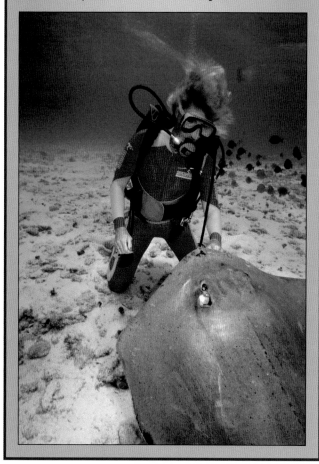

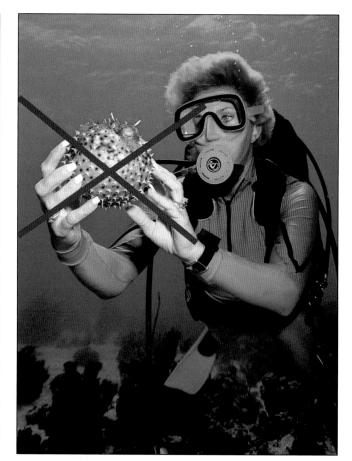

Times have changed, and diver interaction with animals must minimize the animal's stress.

handled or harassed various animals just for the sake of a picture. It was common to see a photo of a puffed up puffer fish, or a sea horse wrapped around someone's finger.

Thankfully, more divers have learned the code of ethics that the reef comes first. If you don't like the location an animal calls home, swim on and find another. There is no call for threatening an animal for the sake of a photo. The underwater photographer can still take pictures and enjoy the creatures of the sea without causing them harm.

■ RULES OF RESPECT

Over the years, we too have evolved as underwater photographers and have had to embrace these new concepts of reef protection. We have gone one step further and devised as system we think will enable all underwater photographers to do their part.

We call our rules for respect "ROY"—respect for the (R)eef, respect for (O)ther photographers, and respect for (Y)ourself. Up to now, we have concentrated our discussion on respecting the reef and its inhabitants. There needs to be respect for other photographers as well. That can be as simple a gesture as not getting too close to another photographer and ruining their shot, or sharing a cool animal that you have discovered.

The third part of ROY is that you must respect yourself. This means that you dive safely and don't let underwater photography get the best of you. With the introduction of larger digital-camera memory cards, you can dive long beyond the old 36 exposures. Today, it's possible to run out of air long before you run out of card memory, so dive sensibly and enjoy being an underwater photographer.

17. Traveling With Your Camera

With the heightened airport security and luggage-weight restrictions, traveling today with underwater photography equipment can be a real challenge. The success of your digital dive trip may hinge on how well you prepare for the trip.

■ ANALYZE THE DIVE LOCATION

Before you even consider packing your gear, you want to analyze what types of photos you will be taking at the dive location. Some dive areas in the world lean more towards wide-angle, fish, macro, or current diving. Knowing your shooting environment will help you eliminate any unnecessary equipment.

■ BACKUP SYSTEMS

Dive trips today can be a very expensive proposition, so try to anticipate any equipment problems you might encounter and be prepared with a backup plan. Each underwater photographer should have one backup camera system, just in case. It doesn't have to be the same camera system, although that is the best plan. It should just be one that will allow you to get some great underwater shots, so you can still enjoy your trip.

This is especially true if you plan on taking an SLR housing system. These systems can be very bulky, so taking two is often impossible due to space and weight restrictions. We recommend that you take an underwater point & shoot camera as your backup system. Just make sure they both take the same memory cards, so you don't have to take too many extra cards along. An advantage to this backup point & shoot camera is that you can use it for topside photographs instead of removing your SLR from the housing.

■ STORING YOUR IMAGES

We recommend that you have two different methods of storing your digital-camera images. Your backup could be in the form of extra memory cards or a laptop computer with enough storage space for your images. We use a portable CD writer that allows us to insert our memory cards directly, without needing a computer. We then burn two copies and carry them home separately. You should also check with the dive location to see if they have equipment for downloading and storing images. If you are traveling with a friend, you can both share a single backup system. Sadly, we have seen sys-

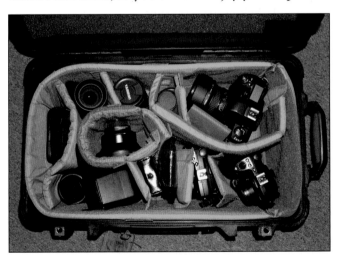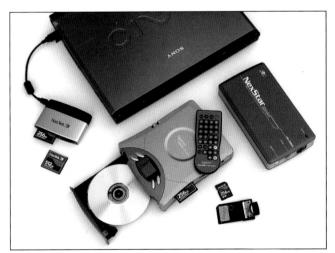

LEFT—Digital cameras are very fragile, so pack them carefully with padding, and take them on the plane as carry-on luggage. Your underwater housings should be packed with the same care, but can be shipped as checked luggage. RIGHT—Take a backup system that allows you to store your digital camera files in two locations. A small laptop and portable CD burner are two good choices.

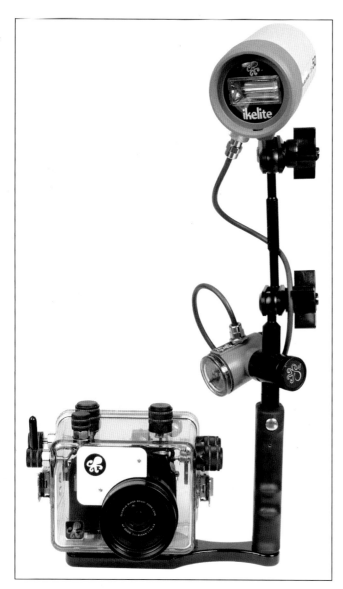

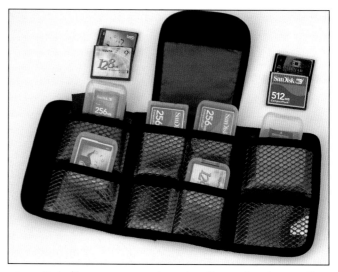

LEFT—Put all you camera systems together and make sure they work before you pack. (Photo courtesy of Ikelite). RIGHT—Several manufacturers now make special carrying cases for memory cards and batteries.

tems fail, and if you don't have a method for backing up your data, you will be limited to the storage space you have on your memory cards.

ADVANCE TESTING

Before packing, you should put both your primary and your backup systems together, to make sure you have all the parts and that everything works. Take several images using wide-angle, normal, and close-up settings. If you find something doesn't work, or you are missing a part, you still have time to fix the problem. You should do this well before your departure date, so there will still be time to get any parts fixed or replaced.

Once your system is put together and working properly, collect all the supporting gear and lay it next to each system. Grab those extra o-rings, batteries,

chargers, battery checkers, camera accessories, lenses, and everything necessary to make your trip a success. Make a list of the items you have laid out and keep a copy for later dive trips.

INSTRUCTION MANUALS

Film shooters usually knew their camera well by the time they left on their dive trip, so instruction manuals weren't always necessary. Digital cameras are a different story. There are few digital photographers who can tell you the location of every control on their camera and how it works. Bring the manual; it may save your trip if you get an error message you've never seen before.

PACKING YOUR GEAR

When you pack your underwater systems, make sure you remove your digital camera from the housing and pack it in a smaller camera bag to carry on the plane. These wonders of the 21st century are very fragile and may not survive as checked luggage. Film shooters should do the same, if for no other reason than most cameras move slightly in the housing when shipped, which can reduce the integrity of the housing itself.

FILM AND X-RAY MACHINES

Under no circumstances should you put your film in your checked luggage, as the x-ray machines used to scan this luggage will permanently fog your film. Take film as a carry-on and have it hand checked if possible. You will need to add an extra half hour to your preboarding time to compensate for having your film checked. Some airports make it so difficult to do that it may not be worth it. After extensive testing, we have found that, in most cases, films ISO 400 and lower can be run through the carry-on x-ray machine with no ill effect. We still recommend that you process a test roll when you get to your location to verify that the film safely made it through the x-ray machine, and that your camera is working properly.

Digital camera users don't have to worry as digital cameras, lenses, and memory cards are unaffected by x-ray machines.

■ LUGGAGE AND WEIGHT RESTRICTIONS

The weight restrictions on airlines seem to change from year to year, so by the time this book is out, they may have changed again. The current limit is two bags at 50 pounds each within the United States, and 70 pounds internationally. Make sure that you are a bit under on each bag, as the airlines tend to watch luggage weight closely. We have even resorted to packing a small fish scale so we have a method of checking the weight for the return trip.

If you find your bags over the weight limit, see if there is anything that can be left behind without jeopardizing the dive trip, otherwise check with the airlines on the cost of taking an extra bag. If you pay for an extra bag, make sure that it flies on the same plane—otherwise it may not catch up to you.

■ INSURANCE

Before you travel, make a list of serial numbers of the equipment you're taking on the trip. Leave one copy at home and take a second with you—but don't store it with the equipment. Insurance coverage for camera equipment varies between companies and, often, is a rider attached to your household coverage. We use one that has a dollar limit on how much we can take on a trip, but is flexible because it doesn't require specific item names or numbers.

■ CHECK AGAIN

When you reach your dive location, look through all the camera gear closely to ensure that it all survived the trip. If you have an acrylic or clear housing, look at the areas near the clamps that secure the housing. A severe shock in travel could force the clamp's screws to fracture the housing. Put your system together as soon as possible, so you can verify that it is working properly. Once assembled, put the system in the fresh-water dunk tank to see if you find any immediate leaks.

If you have a new housing that has never been wet, we recommend that you take an empty housing down on your first checkout dive. Grease the O-rings, but leave the camera out. This is just a way to guarantee you have a great dive trip.

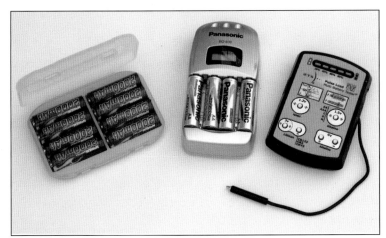 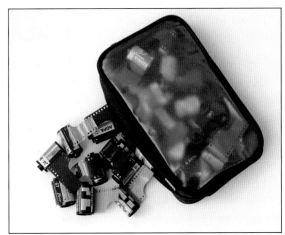

LEFT—Make sure you take plenty of batteries, chargers, and even a battery-load tester. Ship all your batteries together—and consider these handy cases that firmly hold batteries in place. RIGHT—If you are a film shooter, take all your film out of the boxes and place the rolls in a clear bag so that airport inspection goes smoothly.

18. Care of Your Underwater Equipment

A cleaning and repair kit should be part of every underwater system. It should contain cotton swabs, O-ring grease, an O-ring remover, wrench set, Swiss army knife–type tool, small work cloth, lens-cleaning tissue, small flashlight, and a magnifier. We use a magnified headset, which allows us to closely view problems areas and O-ring surfaces and still keep both hands free. There have been many times when we have found problem hairs and particles on the O-ring that we couldn't see without the magnification.

■ MAINTENANCE OF O-RINGS

When you put your system together to test before your dive trip, you should use a magnifier to check all O-ring surfaces and threaded screws that secure the system together. We put a bit of grease on all threaded surfaces to ensure that they move smoothly and to reduce any corrosion that occurs from contact with saltwater.

■ GREASING O-RINGS

As we noted previously, there has been a lot of controversy on how much grease to put on O-rings and how often to put it on. Everyone you ask seems to offer a different solution. So, what do you do?

Here's our story. During our 35 years of underwater photography, we had one Nikonos flood and one digital camera flood. The Nikonos failed because of a faulty O-ring inside the lens that we could not have prevented. The digital flood came because of a design flaw in a point & shoot housing. We feel our success (knock on wood) of having only minimal flooding is due to our consistent method for O-ring maintenance.

Before each trip, we remove each O-ring that is normally maintained, and remove all the grease using a clean lint-free cloth. We then examine the O-ring surface using our magnified headset to check for hairs and sand particles. We apply a small amount of grease on the O-ring so that it slips easily through our fingers as we feel for any irregularities. We clean the groove with a cotton swab, put the O-ring back in place, then check it again using the magnifier.

When preparing for a dive, we again use the headset viewer to verify that the O-ring surface is properly greased and free of dirt. If the O-ring is a little dry, we add a small amount of grease over the surface without removing the O-ring, and immediately close the housing. Every three days we strip down the entire system, removing the serviceable O-rings to clean and regrease them. If our camera housing is ever set down in mud or sand, we service the housing before the next dive.

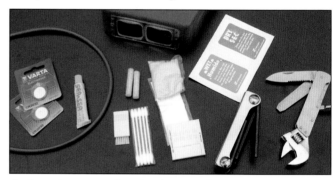

An important part of caring for your digital camera system is preparing a cleaning and repair kit for both the camera and the housing.

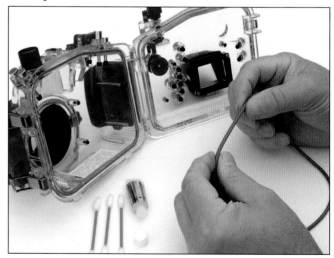

Standardize the way you grease your O-rings. Don't overdo it, and don't stop in the middle of the process.

Contrary to popular belief, putting too much grease on an O-ring doesn't flood your camera; rather it is the dust, hair, and particles the grease attracts that cause the problem. Therefore, you should close the back of your housing immediately after greasing its O-ring—the longer you wait, the more chance you will have trouble as the grease attracts dust.

Be sure that, when you are cleaning your housing and O-rings, you maintain your focus on the problem at hand. We have seen several housings flood because their owners were engaged in conversation and forgot to replace an O-ring.

■ KEEP IT DRY

When you lean over to work on your camera system, it is critical that your hair, head, arms, and upper body be dry. It wasn't as critical with film cameras, as a small drop of water in the housing was not a big deal. Digital cameras are loaded with electronics, though, and the slightest amount of salt water can destroy a camera. If you lean over a digital camera while wearing a wet suit, a small drop could easily fall on the digital camera back, slide through a small crack, flow onto the circuit board and be the death of your camera. Take time to remove your suit, dry your upper torso, and then work with your camera.

Another critical aspect of water in digital cameras is heat. If you drop a very small amount of water in the housing and it goes undetected, you may be in for trouble. Digital cameras generate an enormous amount of heat during a dive, and a small drop of water will vaporize and form a small storm cloud inside your housing. This cloud will then seep into your camera's electronics.

Most underwater digital cameras today come with a desiccant gel pack that can be placed in the housing to absorb any moisture during the dive. We have even seen point & shoot housings with special slots on the housing walls designed to hold these gel packs. Make sure to bring them and use them on your dive trip.

■ CAMERA RINSE TANKS

Most dive locations and live-aboard dive boats today have rinse tanks designated for camera gear. We are amazed at how many photographers will leave their system sitting in these tanks for long periods of time. The largest percentages of floods we have seen in the last 35 years have come from damage while in rinse tanks. Cameras and housing are constantly being dropped in, banged around and then removed. When you come up from a dive, put your system in the rinse tank. Swish it up and down and back and forth three to six times. Remove it from the tank and you will find that almost 90 percent of the saltwater will have been removed.

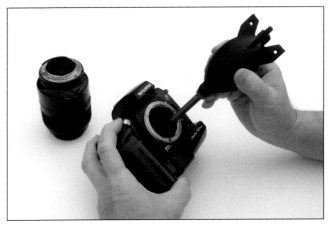

Digital SLRs will eventually collect dirt on the CCD. The best way to clean them is to put the camera on a slow, manual shutter speed and use an air blower to gently clean the sensor.

19. The Future of Underwater Photography

We have heard several professionals express their concern that digital photography now allows everyone to take great pictures underwater. It's true that the digital camera provides high-quality images, but a good image still relies on the trained eye behind the viewfinder or LCD viewer. If the underwater photographer doesn't have a good grasp of the concepts of focus, exposure, and framing, they're not going to do any better than with film. The only difference between film and digital underwater photographers is that the digital photographers can take more bad pictures.

When asked about where underwater photography is headed, we have to say that film will be around for a while, but digital is here to stay. If you are debating whether to stay with film or take the plunge into digital, think about the environmental impact. Film has long been one of the largest sources of pollution on the planet, from its emulsion manufacturers to its processing pollutants. So, if you are considering going to digital and need a reason, do it for the environment.

We have converted to 100 percent digital, both topside and underwater, and love the added control digital provides. Once we learn a new system, we find that we are able to devote all our dive time to the creative aspects of our photography. Even if we have dived at a location before while shooting film, we feel like we are starting all over again with digital—and it's so exciting!

We are still scanning our 100,000+ film images and will continue to do so for the next few years. Our goal is to eventually convert all our film images to digital so then we can intermix them with our digital-camera images. There will come a day when we finally say goodbye to our film world and put it to rest. Until then, we will continue to take advantage of all the potential the underwater digital world has to offer.

Have a good dive, and we hope our book will help you take some great underwater digital photos.

Adobe Photoshop—www.adobe.com

Andromeda LensDoc—www.andromeda.com

Aquatica—www.aquatica.ca

Backscatter—www.backscatter.com

Bilikiki Cruises—www.bilikiki.com

Bonica—www.bonicadive.com

Brooks Institute of Photography—
www.brooksinstitute.edu

Canon—www.usa.canon.com

Capt. Don's Habitat—www.habitatbonaire.com

Dfine—www.nikmultimedia.com

Digideep—www.digideep.com

Digital Diver—www.digitaldiver.net

Digital GEM—www.asf.com

Digital Photo—www.digitalphoto.net

Digital Photography Review—www.dpreview.com

Epoque—www.epoque-usa.com

Focus Magic—www.focusmagic.com

Fuji—www.fujifilm.com

Genuine Print Pro—www.lizardtech.com

Ikelite—www.ikelite.com

INON—www.inonamerica.com

Jack and Sue Drafahl—www.jackandsuedrafahl.com

Kodak—www.kodak.com

Konica Minolta—www.konicaminolta.com

Lexar—www.lexar.com

Light & Motion Industries—www.lmionline.com

Marine Camera Distributors—www.marinecamera.com

Mystical Lighting—www.autofx.com

Nai'a Cruises—www.naia.com.fi

Nexus—www.nexusamerica.com

Nikon—www.nikonusa.com

Olympus—www.olympus.com

Oregon Coast Digital Center—
www.oregoncoastdigitalcenter.com

Pelican Products—www.pelican.com

Pentax—www.pentax.com

San Disk—www.sandisk.com

Sea & Sea Underwater—www.seaandsea.com

Seacam—www.seacamusa.com

Sealife—www.sealife-cameras.com

SmartScale—www.extensis.com

Sony—www.sony.com

Subal—www.subal.com

Sunset House Resort—www.sunsethouse.com

UK-GERMANY—www.uk-germany.com

Ultralight Control Systems—www.ulcs.com

Underwater Photo-Tech—www.uwphoto.com

Underwater Society of America—
www.underwater-society.org.

Wet Pixel—www.wetpixel.com

Women Divers Hall of Fame—www.wdhof.org

Index

A

Advance testing, 118
Air bubbles, 44
Analog photography, 6, 15–16
Aperture, 48, 50–51
Arms, camera, 20–21
Available-light photography, 54–60
 blooming, 56
 camera angle, 56
 color balance, 55
 deep water, 59–60
 exposure methods, 55
 flashlights as props with, 60
 point of view, 55–56
 shallow water, 59
 silhouettes, 55–56
 white balance, 59

B

Backscatter, 8–9, 100–106
 causes of, 101–3
 extreme, 104–6
 flash distance to camera,
  100–101
 lighting contrast, 102–3
 software solutions, 106
 subject distance to camera,
  101–2
Backup systems, 117
Batteries
 charging, 26
 flash, 65
 Lithium Ion, 26
 Ni-MH, 26
 traveling with, 26–27
Black & white mode, 38–39, 59
Blooming, 33, 47–48, 56
Brackets, camera, 20–21

C

Camera arms, 20–21
Camera brackets, 20–21
Cameras, digital
 advantages of, 13–15
 batteries, 26–27
 CCD, 15, 25–26, 48
 CMOS, 15, 25–26
 before buying, 12–13
 components, 23–27
 exposure, see Exposure
 file compression, 37
 focusing, see Focusing
 hot shoe, 24, 34
 ISO speeds, 14–15, 30–31
 knob labels, 21–22
 LCD display, 24
 LCD menus, 21–22, 24
 memory cards, 26
 menus, see Menus, digital
  camera
 number of exposures, 13
 optical viewfinder, 23
 point & shoot, 17
 practicing with topside, 41
 researching, 22
 resolution, 37
 SLR, 17
 traveling with, 13–14, 120–21
 vs. film cameras, 17
 white balance, 15, 28–30
Cameras, film
 advantages of, 15–16
 vs. digital cameras, 17
CCD chip, 15, 25–26, 48
Close-up photography, 86–93; see
  also Super macro
  photography

(Close-up photography, cont'd)
 depth of field, 91–93
 diopters, 88–89
 extension tubes, 87–88
 flash with, 90–91
 focusing, 35–36
 frame enhancers, 91
 framers, 87–88
 macro lenses, SLR, 88
 terminology, 87
 with point & shoot cameras,
  89–90
CMOS chip, 15, 25–26
Color
 saturation, 8, 9, 15, 33
 spectrum, 8, 9
Composition, 39, 107–13
 busy scenes, 112
 color, 109
 cropping, 111
 framing, 111
 grid, 39
 leading lines, 108–9
 letter compositions, 111
 light traps, 112
 negative space, 109–10
 opposites attract, 110
 patterns and shapes, 111
 point of view, 111
 rule of thirds, 107–8
 subject position, 112
Continuous-shooting mode, 36–37
Contrast, 8, 15, 32–33
Corrosion, 10–11
Currents, 10

D

Deleting images, 45

Depth of field, 91–93
    software solutions, 93
    subject angles, 93
    with point & shoot models, 92
Diopters, 19, 22, 88–89, 96–97

E
EXIF metadata, 37–38, 45
Exposure
    aperture, 48, 50–51
    blooming, 33, 47–48, 56
    bracket, 34–35
    compensation, 33–34
    ISO setting, 14–15, 30–31, 49
    latitude, 53
    manual, 40
    modes, *see* Exposure Modes
    problems with, 21–22
    shutter speed, 48–49, 51–53
    testing, 47–48
Exposure Modes
    aperture-priority, 50–51
    manual, 40, 53
    program, 43, 49–50
    shutter-priority, 51–53

F
Face mask, 21–22
File
    compression, 37
    naming, 39–40
Filters, warming, 55
Firmware updates, 27
Fish photography, 78–85
    analog photography, 78–80
    animal behavior, 84–85
    cleaning stations, 85
    digital photography 80–85
    flash considerations, 82–84
    point & shoot images, 81
    SLR images, 81–82
    techniques for, 84–85
Flash, 8, 18, 20–21, 24, 32, 33–35, 43–44, 61–69
    arms, 20–21, 69

(*Flash, cont'd*)
    automatic, 69
    batteries, 65
    brackets, 20–21
    close-up images with, 90–91
    color, effect on, 8
    digital, 63
    exposure, 33–35, 61–62
    fish photography with, 82–84
    flash-sync port, 34
    flash-to-subject distance, 8
    high-speed, 64, 90–91
    hot shoe, 24, 34
    positioning, 43–44
    manual, 63
    port-mounted, 63
    recycle time, 65–66
    single, 66
    slaved, 34, 64, 68
    slow, 32
    synchronization, 18, 34, 63–64
    TTL, 18, 62–64
    TTL housing control boards, 65
    twin, 63, 66–67
    wide-angle, 67–68
Flashlights, 19–20, 60
    as props, 60
Focusing, 21–22, 35–36
    brackets, 34
    close-up mode, 35–36
    continuous, 35
    problems with, 21–22
    software solutions, 93
    super macro mode, 36

G
Grain, *see* Noise

H
Histogram, 37–38
Housings
    air bubbles between lens and, 44
    maintenance of, 41–43, 120–21
    O-rings, greasing, 41–43
    overheating, 26

(*Housings, cont'd*)
    practicing with, 41
    test dive with, 42
Humidity, 10–11

I
Instruction manuals, 118
Insurance, 119
ISO speeds
    for super macro photography, 98
    noise, 14, 30–31
    variety of, 14–15, 30–31, 49

J
JPEG format, 37

L
LCD display, 24, 40, 45
Lenses
    accessory, 18–19, 37
    air bubbles between housings and, 44
    diopters, 19, 88–89
    extension tubes, 87–88
    fisheye, 37
    focusing, 21–22, 35–36
    framers, 87–88
    macro, 88
    tele-extenders, 96
    wet, 18–19, 71, 97–98
    wide-angle, 70–77
    zoom, digital *vs.* optical, 40
Lighting
    available light, *see* Available-light photography
    color, 8
    flash, *see* Flash
    flashlights, 19–20
    light loss, 8
Luggage, weight restrictions, 119

M
Magnifying glass, 99
Maintenance of equipment, 120–21

Manual exposure, 40
Memory cards
    changing, 27
    number of images on, 12–13,
        27, 37
    size of, 27, 37
    types of, 27
Menus, digital camera
    black & white mode, 38–39
    composition grid, 39
    Continuous-shooting mode,
        36–37
    contrast, 32–33
    custom presets, 38
    default settings, 28
    EXIF metadata, 37–38, 45
    exposure bracket, 34–35
    exposure compensation, 33–34
    file compression, 37
    file naming, 39–40
    flash, 31–32
    focus, 35–36
    ISO speeds, 30–31
    LCD monitor control, 40
    manual exposure, 40
    noise reduction, 38
    panoramic mode, 38
    program mode, 43
    resolution, 37
    sepia mode, 38–39
    set-up, 40
    sharpness, 32
    video, 39
    white balance, 28–30
Metadata, 37–38, 45
Models, working with, 75

N
Noise, digital, 14, 30–31, 32
    effect of sharpening, 32
    noise-reduction camera setting,
        38
    reducing with software, 31

O
Overheating, 26

P
Panoramic images, 38, 77
Program mode, 43

R
RAW format, 37
Reefs, protecting, 114–16
    animals, interacting with, 116
    buoyancy skills, 114–15
    dead zones, 115
    ethics, 115–16
    time outs, 115
Resolution, 37
Rinse tanks, 121

S
Saturation, color, 8, 9, 15, 33
Self portraits, 75–76
Sepia mode, 38–39
Sharpening, in-camera, 32
Shipwrecks, 14, 59, 74, 104
Shutter speed, 48–49, 51–53
Silhouettes, 55
Sound recording, 37
Super macro photography, 94–99
    auxiliary lights, 98
    definition of, 95
    diopters, 96–97
    face-mask configurations, 99
    ISO, 98
    software magnification, 99
    techniques for, 95–96
    tele-extenders, 96
    wet lens, 97–98
    with point & shoot cameras, 97

T
Temperature of water, 9–10
TIF format, 37
Time-lapse photography, 36–37

Traveling with your camera,
    117–21
Trays, 69

V
Video mode, 39

W
Water
    column, reducing, 71–72
    temperature, 9–10
White balance, 28–30, 34, 59
    auto, 28, 29
    available-light images and, 59
    below 30 feet, 30
    bracketing, 34
    cloudy, 29
    custom, 29, 30
    fluorescent, 29
    shade, 29
    shallow-water images and, 69
    sunlight, 29
Wide-angle photography, 70–77
    camera angles, 72–73
    digital lens configurations,
        70–71
    models, working with, 75
    panoramic images, 38, 77
    perspective, 73–74
    self portraits, 75–76
    shipwrecks, 74–75
    water column, reducing, 71–72
    wet lenses, 71

X
X-ray machines, 118–19

Z
Zoom, digital *vs.* optical, 40

OTHER BOOKS FROM
Amherst Media®

Also by Jack and Sue Drafahl . . .

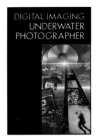

DIGITAL IMAGING FOR THE UNDERWATER PHOTOGRAPHER, 2nd Ed.

This book will teach readers how to improve their underwater images with digital image-enhancement techniques. This book covers all the bases—from color balancing your monitor, to scanning, to output and storage. $39.95 list, 6x9, 224p, 240 color photos, order no. 1727.

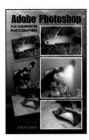

ADOBE® PHOTOSHOP®
FOR UNDERWATER PHOTOGRAPHERS

In this sequel to *Digital Imaging for the Underwater Photographer,* the Drafahls show you advanced techniques for solving a wide range of image problems that are unique to underwater photography. $39.95 list, 6x9, 224p, 100 color photos, 120 screen shots, index, order no. 1825.

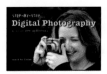

STEP-BY-STEP DIGITAL PHOTOGRAPHY, 2nd Ed.

Avoiding the complexity and jargon of most manuals, this book will quickly get you started using your digital camera to create memorable photos. $14.95 list, 9x6, 112p, 185 color photos, index, order no. 1763.

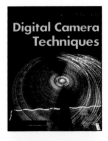

ADVANCED DIGITAL CAMERA TECHNIQUES

Maximize the quality and creativity of your digital-camera images with the techniques in this book. Packed with problem-solving tips and ideas for unique images. $29.95 list, 8½x11, 128p, 150 color photos, index, order no. 1758.

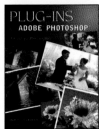

PLUG-INS FOR ADOBE® PHOTOSHOP®
A GUIDE FOR PHOTOGRAPHERS

Supercharge your creativity and mastery over your photography with Photoshop and the tools outlined in this book. $29.95 list, 8½x11, 128p, 175 color photos, index, order no. 1781.

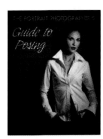

THE PORTRAIT PHOTOGRAPHER'S GUIDE TO POSING
Bill Hurter

Posing can make or break an image. Now you can get the posing tips and techniques that have propelled the finest portrait photographers in the industry to the top. $34.95 list, 8½x11, 128p, 200 color photos, index, order no. 1779.

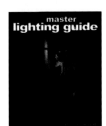

MASTER LIGHTING GUIDE
FOR PORTRAIT PHOTOGRAPHERS
Christopher Grey

Efficiently light executive and model portraits, high and low key images, and more. Master traditional lighting styles and use creative modifications that will maximize your results. $29.95 list, 8½x11, 128p, 300 color photos, index, order no. 1778.

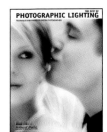

THE BEST OF PHOTOGRAPHIC LIGHTING
Bill Hurter

Top professionals reveal the secrets behind their successful strategies for studio, location, and outdoor lighting. Packed with tips for portraits, still lifes, and more. $34.95 list, 8½x11, 128p, 150 color photos, index, order no. 1808.

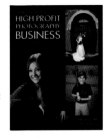

HOW TO CREATE A HIGH PROFIT PHOTOGRAPHY BUSINESS
IN ANY MARKET
James Williams

Whether your studio is located in a rural or urban area, you'll learn to identify your ideal client type, create the images they want, and watch your financial and artistic dreams spring to life! $34.95 list, 8½x11, 128p, 200 color photos, index, order no. 1819.

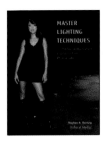

MASTER LIGHTING TECHNIQUES
FOR OUTDOOR AND LOCATION DIGITAL PORTRAIT PHOTOGRAPHY
Stephen A. Dantzig

Use natural light alone or with flash fill, bare-bulb, and strobes to shoot perfect portraits all day long. $34.95 list, 8½x11, 128p, 175 color photos, diagrams, index, order no. 1821.

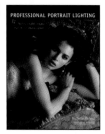

PROFESSIONAL PORTRAIT LIGHTING

TECHNIQUES AND IMAGES FROM MASTER PHOTOGRAPHERS

Michelle Perkins

Get a behind-the-scenes look at the lighting techniques employed by the world's top portrait photographers. $34.95 list, 8½x11, 128p, 200 color photos, index, order no. 2000.

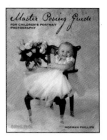

MASTER POSING GUIDE

FOR CHILDREN'S PORTRAIT PHOTOGRAPHY

Norman Phillips

Create perfect portraits of infants, tots, kids, and teens. Includes techniques for standing, sitting, and floor poses for boys and girls, individuals, and groups. $34.95 list, 8½x11, 128p, 305 color images, order no. 1826.

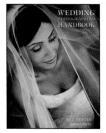

WEDDING PHOTOGRAPHER'S HANDBOOK

Bill Hurter

Learn to produce images with unprecedented technical proficiency and superb, unbridled artistry. Includes images and insights from top industry pros. $34.95 list, 8½x11, 128p, 180 color photos, 10 screen shots, index, order no. 1827.

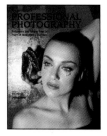

RANGEFINDER'S PROFESSIONAL PHOTOGRAPHY

edited by Bill Hurter

Editor Bill Hurter shares over one hundred "recipes" from *Rangefinder's* popular cookbook series, showing you how to shoot, pose, light, and edit fabulous images. $34.95 list, 8½x11, 128p, 150 color photos, index, order no. 1828.

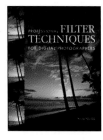

PROFESSIONAL FILTER TECHNIQUES

FOR DIGITAL PHOTOGRAPHERS

Stan Sholik

Select the best filter options for your photographic style and discover how their use will affect your images. $34.95 list, 8½x11, 128p, 150 color images, index, order no. 1831.

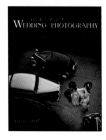

MASTER'S GUIDE TO WEDDING PHOTOGRAPHY

CAPTURING UNFORGETTABLE MOMENTS AND LASTING IMPRESSIONS

Marcus Bell

Learn to capture the unique energy and mood of each wedding and build a lifelong client relationship. $34.95 list, 8½x11, 128p, 200 color photos, index, order no. 1832.

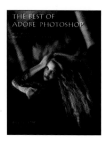

THE BEST OF ADOBE® PHOTOSHOP®

Bill Hurter

Rangefinder editor Bill Hurter calls on the industry's top photographers to share their strategies for using Photoshop to intensify and sculpt their images. No matter your specialty, you'll find inspiration here. $34.95 list, 8½x11, 128p, 170 color photos, 10 screen shots, index, order no. 1818.

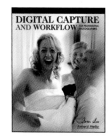

MASTER LIGHTING GUIDE

FOR COMMERCIAL PHOTOGRAPHERS

Robert Morrissey

Learn to use the tools and techniques the pros rely upon to land corporate clients. Includes diagrams, images, and techniques for a failsafe approach to creating shots that sell. $34.95 list, 8½x11, 128p, 110 color photos, 125 diagrams, index, order no. 1833.

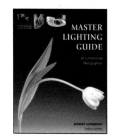

DIGITAL CAPTURE AND WORKFLOW

FOR PROFESSIONAL PHOTOGRAPHERS

Tom Lee

Cut your image-processing time by fine-tuning your workflow. Includes tips for working with Photoshop and Adobe Bridge, plus framing, matting, and more. $34.95 list, 8½x11, 128p, 150 color images, index, order no. 1835.